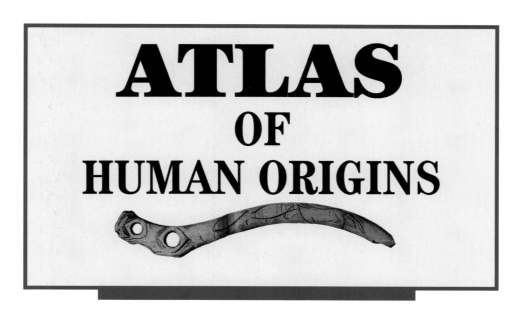

ATLAS
OF
HUMAN ORIGINS

Written by
Henri de Saint-Blanquat

Illustrated by
Benoît Clarys

BARRON'S

SCIENTIFIC ADVISORS

- **Dominique Baffier,** Engineer, Prehistoric Ethnology Laboratory, CNRS (National Center for Scientific Research)

- **Pascal Picq,** Assistant Professor, College de France,

- **Jean-Jacques Hublin,** Director of Research, CNRS.

Art Director

Giampiero Caiti/Millefeuilles

Acknowledgments

The author, the illustrator, and the editor thank

the Malgré-Tout Museum, Tregnes;

Anne Hauzeur, Yvan Jadin and Patrick Semal (Royal Institute of Natural Sciences, Belgium);

Herbert Thomas, Michel Lorblanchet, Bernard Vandermeersch and Jacques Cauvin for their precious documents.

Photo credits

p. 4: L. Psihoyos Matrix/Cosmos; p. 9: H. Thomas; p. 12: E. Ferorelli/Cosmos; p. 12–13, 17, 24, 27: J. Reader-Science Photo Library/Cosmos; p. 19: Ph. De Foy/Explorer; p. 26: M. Denis-Huot/Hoa Qui; p. 33: Ch. O'Rear/Cosmos; p. 35 top: J. Trueba/Madrid Scientific Films; p. 35 middle, 36 bottom, 37: DR; p. 36 top, 47 bottom, 56, 68, 69, 70, 75: J-M Labat/Casterman Archives; p. 39: Museum of Man/Casterman Archives; p. 41: D. Vaughan-Science Photo Library/Cosmos; p. 43, 72 top, 72 middle: Casterman Archives/DR; p. 47 top: B. Hatala/Museum of Man; p. 50 top, 53: B. Vandermeersch; p. 54: J. Oster/Museum of Man; p. 58: J.-L. Klein/Pix; p. 59, 73, 84 top: M. Lorblanchet; p. 60: A. Chéné; p. 61 top: Th. Stephan/Ulmer Museum; p. 61 middle, 66, 74: J. Vertut; p. 62: D. Lehman/Westlight/Cosmos; p. 65: Ditges/Explorer; p. 72 bottom: M. Girard/G. De la Varende collection; p. 76: Dagli Orti; p. 77 top: P. Boulat/Cosmos; p. 77 bottom: G. Boutin/Explorer; p. 78 top: J.-L. Bohin/Explorer; p. 79: B. Guiter/Explorer; p. 80: Th. Wiewandt/Pix; p. 83: Th. Mauger/Explorer; p. 84 bottom: P. Leroux/Explorer; p. 85: J.-P. Ferrero/Explorer; p. 86 and 87: J. Cauvin.

The drawings on pages 48–49 are reproduced with the permission of the Walloon Region; those on pages 25, 51, 55, 66–67, 69, 92 with the permission of the Royal Museums of Art and of History, Brussels.

First edition for the United States and Canada published 1999 by Barron's Educational Series, Inc.
English translation © copyright 1999 by Barron's Educational Series, Inc.

© copyright 1998 by CASTERMAN, Tournai-Belgium, for the original version.

All inquiries should be addressed to:
Barron's Educational Series, Inc.
250 Wireless Boulevard
Hauppauge, New York 11788
http://www.barronseduc.com

Library of Congress Catalog Card No.: 99-20657
International Standard Book No.: 0-7641-5190-8

Library of Congress Cataloging-in-Publication Data
  Saint-Blanquat, Henri de.
      [Atlas de premiers hommes. English]
      Atlas of human origins / written by Henri de Saint-Blanquat ; illustrated
  by Benoît Clarys.
          p.   cm.
      Translation of: Atlas des premiers hommes.
      Includes index.
      ISBN 0-7641-5190-8
        1. Human beings—Origin.   2. Fossil hominids.   3. Prehistoric peoples.
  I. Clarys, Benoît, ill.   II. Title.
  GN281.S24313   1999
  599.93'8—dc21   99-20657
                                                        CIP

PRINTED IN BELGIUM
9 8 7 6 5 4 3 2 1

CONTENTS

THE WORLD, 65 MILLION YEARS AGO

A real ocean lay between Europe and Africa, which modern geologists have named for the wife of the Titan Oceanos: Tethys. The Atlantic Ocean? A long sea barely wider than the Mediterranean is today.

Almost another Earth! In Europe, the chain of the Alps did not exist—in its place was a deep, narrow sea—and the Pyrenees mountain chain had just begun to develop. A warm sea covered the Aquitaine. Africa was an area even larger than it is today, but it was still connected to regions that have since detached: Italy, Sicily, Corsica, and Sardinia, and a large portion of the Balkans, as well as all of Arabia, separated from Asia by the Tethys.

A Planet Without Humans

The two Americas remained two separate continents. India, an immense island, had not yet collided with Asia: The Himalayas would result from this formidable collision. And Antarctica was not yet located at the South Pole. Despite a recent cooling, the climate was still hot or warm almost everywhere. It would have been a good time for humans to exist . . . . . But there you have it: Humans did not exist! We have not found a single animal from that time that was either a close or a distant relative.

The End of the Dinosaurs

Nevertheless, the world was alive from the beginnings of the Tertiary period. Earth had barely survived one of the most serious crises it had ever faced. Had anyone traveled across continents, that traveler would have encountered few animals, except for tortoises, snakes, crocodiles, and insects. No horses, no lions, nothing that resembled them.

No Elephants, No Mice

In the skies were birds that were so slow and clumsy that we would hardly recognize them as such. No seals or walruses lived in the seas; no dolphins leapt out of the waters.

Before the Tertiary period, dinosaurs ruled. They lived almost everywhere. Some were no bigger than pigeons. And contrary to what many people believe, they were not all slow and clumsy. *Velociraptor* was so named using two Latin words that mean "fast" and "thief." The remains of one were found alongside the eggs of another dinosaur. When we see the remains of such beings, we may wonder how the animal world would have evolved had a catastrophe not eliminated the dominant elements.

One of our ancestors might have looked like this during the time of the dinosaurs. This small animal, similar to a shrew, may resemble some of the small mammals of the Mesozoic era, pushed out by the dominant dinosaurs.

A SHOWER OF METEORITES

More and more scientists believe that a cataclysm caused the dinosaurs to become extinct, leaving the field open for mammals. The two most common theories of what this disaster was involve the fall of an enormous meteorite, alone or with a series of gigantic volcanic eruptions. Traces of such a meteorite that fell around this time were actually discovered in Mexico (Yucatan) while at the same time in India, lava flows covered millions of square miles. Whatever its cause, a catastrophic event had to have projected considerable quantities of dust into the atmosphere, concealing the sun, quickly cooling the climate, and producing a profound environmental upheaval. The dinosaurs, accustomed to the warm temperatures, could not survive the change or resist other animals, whether on the land or sea.

During the Mesozoic era, a particular group of animals dominated the earthly scene, animals that we are beginning to know quite well: reptiles. The reptiles that lived on land were called dinosaurs, and if we could have visited Earth at the end of the Mesozoic era, dinosaurs are probably the only animal we would have seen. Geologists are still not sure why—perhaps the fall of a giant asteroid, gigantic eruptions, or cooling of the climate—these sovereigns mysteriously disappeared. After their demise, a group of animals that until then were relatively unimportant, even marginal, began to take their place.

Liberated Mammals

Slowly, the world changed. The continents drifted apart at a rate of several centimeters per year. The climate gradually changed and lost the steady warmth that had prevailed for millions of years. It began to fluctuate, and the resulting weather patterns would be marked by more and more severe cooling.

This was the start of the age of other animals—mammals, which is what we are. Mammals are animals that give birth to live offspring, without a protective egg, who nurse them and therefore have mammary glands, and who continuously maintain the same internal body temperature. Mammals had actually existed for tens of millions of years, but they were dominated by reptiles, especially dinosaurs, and so remained small animals, rare and furtive, often nocturnal. Liberated by the demise of the giants, they began to diversify and occupy new ecological niches. They reigned on land everywhere. Among them, a rather curious group would make its appearance: the primates. Their niche seemed to be the trees, which had just begun to sprout leaves and flowers.

It was almost another Earth.

LIVE IN TREES?
WHAT A STRANGE IDEA...

As surprises go, this one was major. Not a single dinosaur remained on Earth. Imagine the emptiness, perhaps the silence . . .

The disappearance of the dinosaurs and many other animals 65 million years ago took the survivors by surprise. The groups that remained took time to recover—to make the most of the opportunity and to occupy all the newly vacated niches. During the first millions of years of the Tertiary period, the living world seemed to pause, still uncertain about the disaster's ultimate outcome. Many animals appeared and vanished, leaving little evidence to tell us what they were. With the large carnivorous quadrupeds gone, birds took their place: large, ferocious running birds, with formidable beaks and claws . . .

A Remarkable Success

Then they arrived: our ancestors. The first evidence of them seems to have appeared at the end of the Mesozoic era with *Purgatorius,* discovered in the United States. Nocturnal and insectivorous, this animal weighed between 3.5 and 5.25 ounces (100–150 g) and must have resembled a shrew, with its slender nose and its pointed teeth. A primate? Probably not, but perhaps similar in appearance to our ancestors at that time. Another group of small arboreal animals, called plesiadapiforms, were also discovered in America. Although some did not weigh more than 1 ounce (30 g), others reached almost 11 pounds (5 kg). They probably resembled our squirrels and many other similar animals because there were more than sixty species of them.

Good Climbers

The plesiadapiforms also lived throughout Europe, perhaps because they were good tree climbers and that region was heavily forested. But these were not true primates: They had claws while almost all primates have nails; their thumbs and big toes were not opposable to the other digits, making it easier to grasp objects, as are those of today's primates.

Lemurs are among the most primitive of living primates. Today they exist only in Madagascar and on the Comoro Islands. Although they do not exactly resemble the earliest primates (they, too, have evolved), their general appearance is very similar. Like the early primate-like beings, they live mostly in trees, where they find most of their food.

Like many of their successors, the first primates lived in trees: They were arboreal. But in which trees? Those that provided both shelter and food, primarily trees with leaves, flowers, and fruits, similar to those in today's large tropical and equatorial forests. The flowering plants (angiosperms, with hidden seeds) had already covered the world for a long time, from the middle of the Jurassic period, approximately 160 million years ago. There were water lilies and palm trees 140 million years ago. At the beginning of the Tertiary period (65 million years ago), the major groups of modern African trees were already present. This makes it very easy to imagine the world of our small, agile ancestors. Color vision, particularly developed in primates, is perhaps connected with hunting for fruit. A single touch was missing in the plant landscape of the time: what we today call "compositae," the group to which thistles, dandelions, and other daisies belong.

to their niche by using nails, opposable thumbs and big toes, a snout, and a somewhat less elongated skull. With the changing environment, a completely new kind of animal lived and reproduced. Without the trees, with their leaves, flowers, and fruit, there would have been no primates and, therefore, no humans.

Living Together

These first primates, the adapids of Asia and the omomyids of Africa, are called "prosimians" and resemble the lemurs of Madagascar and the tarsiers of Asia. One characteristic shared by prosimians of today and their ancestors is the retention of a grooming claw on one of their digits. The first primates led an early and friendly form of social life.

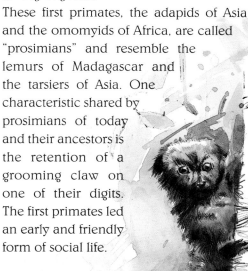

These fossils provide evidence of the existence of an intermediary animal, somewhere between primates and rodents, neither of which existed yet. The ancestor of primates would be better sought in Africa.

The First Primates

The first incontestable primates appeared at the beginning of the Tertiary period, in the Eocene epoch, when the climate became warmer. Leafy trees multiplied and produced savory fruits, and provided shelter and better protection. The first true primates adapted

At the beginning of the Tertiary period, the niches left unoccupied by the large carnivorous dinosaurs were filled by birds, one of which was *Diatryma*. This bird was 7 feet (2 m) tall, with enormous feet and an impressive beak, and lived during the Eocene epoch. The first primates must have seen this large bird. But carnivorous mammals also developed. Because they were more effective predators, they probably eliminated *Diatryma*.

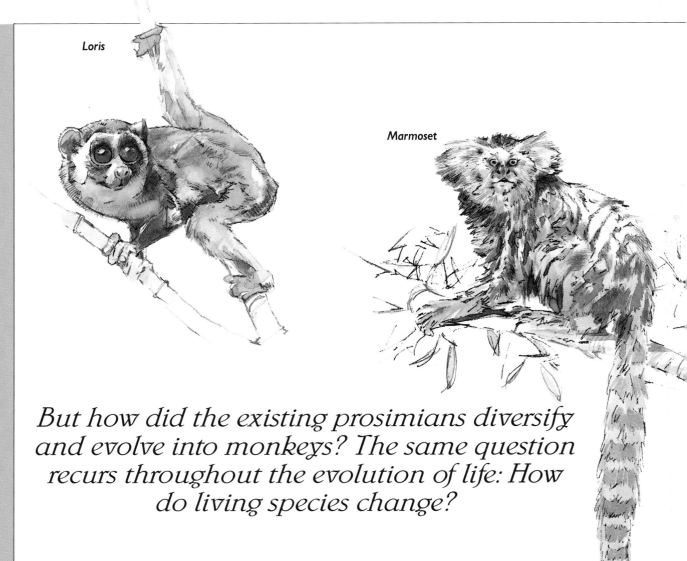

Loris

Marmoset

MONKEYS

But how did the existing prosimians diversify and evolve into monkeys? The same question recurs throughout the evolution of life: How do living species change?

How does one become a primate, monkey, ape, or human? Specialists find this hard to explain. What they see are the differences. They note first the shape of the skull: In monkeys, the cranium is better developed, more round, especially behind the eyes, than in the prosimians. In addition, the monkey's brain is bigger than that of the prosimian.

Everything Changed

In monkeys, some bones in the skull fuse together, whereas in prosimians they remain unfused, especially in the forehead and chin. Monkeys, therefore, do not have the "elastic" chewing ability of their cousins. Monkeys also generally have shorter snouts and no distinguishable "grooming claw" on their feet, only nails. Finally, monkeys have better eyesight than prosimians, but a less refined sense of smell, differences visible in the bones associated with these functions.

The Earliest Monkeys

Although there are bits of jawbone from Burma and Thailand that date back more than 30 million years, the oldest monkey fossils appear from the end of the Eocene epoch. These first monkey remains were found primarily in the two major fossil sites, one in the Fayum of Egypt, the other in Oman in the south of the Arabian peninsula, in the province of Dhofar. *Aegyptopithecus, Parapithecus,* and *Propliopithecus* from Fayum, like *Moeripithecus* from Oman, lived in the warm and humid environment that prevailed in these regions.

Roots in the Water

In Oman, the evidence suggests that these animals lived close to the sea, perhaps in a mangrove swamp. In Fayum, they favored a tropical forest in the marshes.

In both, it appears that the animals needed trees with their roots in the water. Our early monkeys lived in these trees, moving on four feet and jumping from one branch to another. Only rarely did they descend to the ground, and they do not seem to have moved by swinging from the branches. Their food? Fruits, seeds, perhaps vegetable gums, but apparently not leaves. These earliest known monkeys lived approximately 33 million years ago. The two areas where they lived are deserts today.

Better eyesight, a less refined sense of smell . . . and nails on all the digits.

Chimpanzee

Baboon

These pages show a small range of modern primates: the first, the loris, is a prosimian from India, closely related to the lemurs of Madagascar; the second, the marmoset, is a small monkey from South America; the third, the chimpanzee, is a hominoid; the fourth, the baboon, is a cercopithecoid; as for the last . . . we know him well.

Researchers at the Thaytiniti deposit, in Oman, where some of the oldest monkey remains were discovered. Today a desert, the area then was a coastal mangrove forest.

HOW IS DATING DONE?

How do we know if a fossil is 4 or 33 million years old? Generally, scientists determine this by dating a layer of sediment located just above or (better) just below that in which the fossil was discovered. For the periods involved in the history of primates, volcanic rocks are the most easily datable. The proportions—very small—of radioactive elements they contain are measured in more or less minuscule proportions. Since all radioactive elements lose their radioactivity over time, at a known rate, the proportion that remains or that is transformed into another element gives an idea of the time that has elapsed since the formation of the rock—in this case the lava flow or the eruption that covered the fossil grounds.

This small lower jawbone, discovered in 1988 in the sultanate of Oman (south of the Arabian peninsula), was named *Moeripithecus markgrafi*. It is 33 million years old and belongs to one of the oldest known monkeys.

THE GREAT APES, OUR FIRST COUSINS

Millions of years passed. The climate seems to have become warmer, with slight fluctuations and, in Africa, started to become drier. A major event: Tethys is cut off from the East when Arabia and Asia join.

In the East, the Indo-Asian shock took place: The Himalayas grew higher and higher . . . . In Africa, rifts opened and deepened, volcanoes multiplied. These rifts provided access to millions of years of sediments that paleontologists may search more readily for fossils.

The Arrival of the Hominoids
New and still fascinating primates appeared. Among this group are the "lesser apes"—gibbons, siamangs—and the "great apes"—orangutans, gorillas, chimpanzees—and us, the human apes.

Clear-cut Quadrupeds
The oldest known quadrupeds—creatures that used four limbs to walk—lived in eastern Africa approximately 20 million years ago (Miocene epoch). At that time there were already more than twenty species: They must, therefore, have originated much earlier. (Some weighed no more than 6.6 to 8.8 pounds (3–4 kg); others perhaps had already reached the 198 pounds (90 kg) of a female gorilla. Their limbs and their joints suggest that, compared with modern monkeys, they ran less quickly than some, climbed less nimbly than others. They were, however, capable of behavior that was more flexible and varied than all the monkeys we know today. The hot climate allowed them to live in Europe: Evidence of many has been found in the south of France. The recent discovery of a new hominoid in Malawi, the *Morotopithecus*, shows that not all were clear-cut quadrupeds: Already some beings could move by suspending themselves from the branches, that is, by becoming vertical. This tendency pointed to interesting

possibilities for the future: It would not be necessary to stand up straight in order to walk on two feet . . .

The Big Ones and the Others
In comparison with the first monkeys, those from Fayum and Oman, the hominoids appear to have diversified, with some living in the humid tropical forest and others in dry forests. Males and females varied more in size and other traits. We know, by observing modern primates, that a large difference in size between males and females characterizes species in which only one male breeds with females. This "sexual dimorphism" is also visible in the size of the canines. However, fossils show that very different kinds of societies already existed, some with groups that had a male with large canines and much bigger body than the females, others in which the two sexes were rather similar and thus without a harem-type society.

The Baboons' Point of View
Must we see the history of primates as simply a "step" toward humanity? This mistake is made frequently. An objective look at history reveals a different story. In fact, another group appeared shortly after the hominoids. In the mid-Miocene epoch, there were still fewer cercopithecoids in comparison with the hominoids who dominated the scene. However, toward the end of this epoch and at the beginning of the next, the Pliocene, these newcomers multiplied, slowly displacing the hominoids in the savanna regions. They were the victors. This group resembled the ancestors of baboons, hamadryas, and colobines—good runners with snouts and powerful jaws. Little by little, the number of hominoids decreased and their habitat shrank to the tropical and equatorial forest. At this time, there were eighty species of cercopithecoids and only twenty hominoid species. From the baboons' point of view, it would have seemed that humanity was only able to appear *in extremis*, the last-minute offspring of a group in decline . . .

A well-known chimpanzee from the London Zoo was named Consul. The four-legged fossil, now considered the ancestor of contemporary great apes, was baptized Proconsul. In fact, Proconsul exhibits the general characteristics of a climbing quadruped. It lived in eastern Africa 20 million years ago.

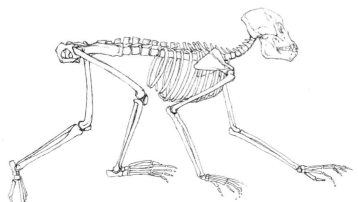

"Hominoids: a name that evokes beings having a vaguely human form."

This is the most impressive of living primates: the gorilla. Males can reach up to 7 feet (2 m) in height and weigh almost 440 pounds (200 kg). Gorillas live deep in the great tropical and equatorial forests of Africa, in small groups consisting of a male and his "harem" of several much smaller females.

Contrary to their popular image, gorillas are very peaceful. In Asia, traces have been found of an even bigger primate: the *Gigantopithecus* (660 lb., or 300 kg).

Here, from top to bottom, are three hominoid fossil skulls: the African *Proconsul*; the more recent Asian *Sivapithecus*, which is probably related to the orangutan; and an *Australopithecus* called "gracile," still more recent and closer to man.

DID YOU SAY PITHECUS? Why all of these bizarre names that end in "pithecus"? One reason is that *pithecos* is the Greek word for "ape." Zoological nomenclature is often constructed using Greek or Latin words so that it is more universal than current languages. Greek has also provided us with *sauros* (lizard) and *anthropos* (man). Latin has given us *Homo* (man), *equus* (horse), *canis* (dog), *felis* (cat), *bos* (ox) . . . . To make the names more precise, they must also be more complex. Thus the dinosaurs are "terrible lizards" (*deinos-sauros*), "sivapithecus" means "Siva's ape," named after the Hindu deity Siva, and the "cercopithecus" are "monkeys with tails." Other names are equally descriptive, such as "australopithecus" (apes from the south), whose remains were found first in southern Africa. One of the first fossil humans that differed from us was initially called "pithecanthropus" (ape-man).

IN AFRICA, MAJOR DISCOVERIES

After the great apes, Australopithecus appeared, the famous "monkeys from the south." Strange beings–and the story of their discovery is no less strange.

The first fossil was found by Dr. Raymond Dart in 1924 in Taung in southern Africa, not Australia ("australo" is Latin for "southern"; hence the name). It was a partial skull and endocast that appeared more human than ape. At the time, however, scientists were skeptical. Many did not agree with the view that it was human but thought it bore more of a resemblance to the great apes. Paleontologists discovered other fossils in the same country, and soon two types became evident, one consisting of "gracile," or slender, beings, the other "robust." Some paleontologists began to wonder whether or not the gracile and robust beings were two distinct lineages.

In the Olduvai Gorge

Then eastern Africa entered the picture. In 1959, Mary Leakey was working in the Olduvai Gorge, in Tanzania, and discovered the skull of an *Australopithecus,* but in the same deposit of sediments she also found simply cut stones. The finding shocked scientists. Were these "worked" stones cut by this type of being? It had to be considered a possibility. But equally surprising was the great age of the fossil, determined by dating one layer of volcanic ash located just below the skull and the stones. Rather than the million years that everyone expected as the fossil's time of origin—and that some already thought too old—the published date was almost double that: These simple pebble tools and the individual without a forehead who may have made them was estimated to be 1,750,000 years old!

The Stone Is the Man

Two years later, at the same site, the Leakeys found another fossil that seemed somewhat closer to modern humans. This being was credited with making the worked stones. Then, in 1964, came the bombshell: the naming of the oldest human fossils from Olduvai. These were human, unquestionably so, dated 1.8 million years before the present. Their name? *Homo habilis,* "handy" men . . . capable and handy because they were the first to make stone tools. We interpret the making of stone tools as a hallmark of being human.

The Rush Toward Human Origins

Enthusiasm poured forth. A wall had fallen, and in doing so, opened a world of possibilities for human origins. Indeed, their origin had been pinpointed. Many projects were organized to explore other deposits. This was a sort of "bone rush," and resulted in many sites becoming famous.

At Laetoli, in Tanzania, older fossils and even footprints were discovered: Two small beings, walking on their two hind legs (bipedal), a small adult and a child, had passed through, leaving their footprints in the ashes, 3.5 million years ago. Then the ground hardened and the tracks of our ancestors were fixed in time and place.

In the Omo valley, in southwest Ethiopia, an international project also found numerous remains of *Australopithecus,* robust and gracile, 2 to 3 million years old. With them they found some small bone fragments of animals living during the same period, but these bone fragments bore the marks of stone tools.

Forty years that changed the origin of humans.

▲ ▲ ▲
A team of researchers at work in Ethiopia.

At Olduvai, in Tanzania, the ▶ geological structure shows ▶ the thick layers of sediment and, consequently, many fossil bones trapped in the sediments.

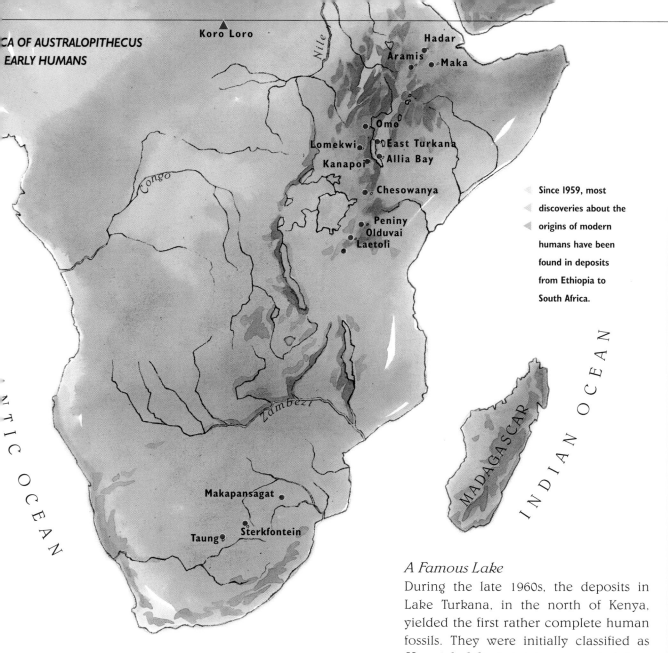

CA OF AUSTRALOPITHECUS
EARLY HUMANS

Koro Loro

Hadar
Aramis   Maka

Omo
Lomekwi   East Turkana
Kanapoi   Allia Bay

Chesowanya

Peniny
Olduvai
Laetoli

Makapansagat

Taung   Sterkfontein

MADAGASCAR

INDIAN OCEAN

ATLANTIC OCEAN

Nile

Congo

Zambezi

Since 1959, most discoveries about the origins of modern humans have been found in deposits from Ethiopia to South Africa.

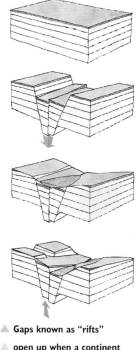

Gaps known as "rifts" open up when a continent begins to divide and form two plates instead of one. This is how Europe slowly separated from North America and Africa from South America. The more the gap deepens, the more the sediments can accumulate and stay, covering and preserving the remains of countless animals . . . and humans. Fortunately for paleontologists, the African rift deepened at the right time, when man was going to be born. They could only regret that the opening had not begun several million years earlier, which would have allowed them to probe the earliest beginnings of human history.

A Famous Lake

During the late 1960s, the deposits in Lake Turkana, in the north of Kenya, yielded the first rather complete human fossils. They were initially classified as *Homo habilis*, but later separated into altogether different species. Today, one of these fossils, similar to the one found in Malawi, is recognized as the oldest known human: *Homo rudolfensis* (Lake Turkana was called Lake Rudolf by the Europeans). These humans lived about 1.8 to 2.4 million years ago. Then in the early 1970s, Lucy was discovered . . .

HOW IDEAS CHANGE! The description of the origin of humans as told today would have made paleontologists of the 1950s laugh. Thus has each discovery eclipsed the previous one. When the first bones of *Homo erectus* were discovered in Java, before 1900, they were thought to be the remains of a being intermediary between apes and man: the *Pithecanthropus* (ape-man). Today we know that these fossils strongly resemble us. In the early 1900s, the skull of a Neanderthal man discovered in Corrèze (in La Chapelle-aux-Saints, France) was studied, and the characteristics that heightened its resemblance to apes were emphasized. Today this man is considered very similar to modern humans, although possibly of another species. This is an ongoing debate, but recent DNA studies suggest that Neanderthals were indeed a species separate from modern humans. And when the first australopithecine discoveries in South Africa were made known in 1925, many specialists refused to see them as anything other than the remains of a new group of great apes. The scientific imagination always saw the origins of modern humans as elsewhere, further back in time.

13

Lucy owes her name to a song by the Beatles, but her fame rests on the fact that she is an exceptional discovery: Never before had paleontologists uncovered so many bones of a fossil that were so close to human.

From Lucy, fifty-two fragments were collected, representing 40 percent of her skeleton. This many bones meant it was possible to know what she looked like. As for her geologic age, the datable volcanic layers in the Ethiopian rift allowed an estimate within 100,000 years.

Quite a Little Person

Thanks to radioactive processes, related to the testing of fossil magnetism, Lucy apparently frolicked in the African region of Ethiopia between 3.10 and 3.22 million years ago. Interesting beings lived there . . . . Their overall size and shape suggested that they were obviously australopithecine, but older than most discovered earlier.

As for Lucy, she must have measured slightly more than 3.5 feet (1 m) in height and weighed about 55 pounds (25 kg). Her skeleton reflects an astonishing mosaic of characteristics: It is as if one had placed in a hat all the characteristics of man and of ape, then pulled some out and used them to construct a strange new organism.

Lucy was born for us on a November day in 1974 . . .

A SMALL BEING **NAMED LUCY**

An Almost Human Pelvis

On the human side, there is the pelvis. Unlike the chimpanzee pelvis, which is narrow and raised when viewed from the front, the human pelvis is low and much wider, designed, in fact, to support the weight of the upright body. The weight of the thorax and abdomen are supported by the pelvis in man; but not in chimpanzees, who have not adopted a vertical posture. The shape of the human pelvis is thus closely linked to walking on two feet. Lucy's pelvis, like ours, is low and broad. From this we can infer that Lucy could hold herself erect and walk efficiently on two feet. Her limbs are certainly those of a bipedal being. The thigh bone (femur) was positioned obliquely, as it is in us, which is key for bipedalism.

But, But . . .

Her legs were somewhat short compared to ours, her arms rather long. In addition, her knee joint was different from ours: It was looser. Similarly, the joint in her shoulders and arms also showed variations. In fact, the joints and the extremities of her limbs very much resemble those of modern chimpanzees. This curious combination suggests that Lucy could both walk and climb trees with agility.

Another Way of Walking

Based on the structure of her pelvis and joints, Lucy did not walk exactly the way we do. She must have had a kind of rolling gait, which was less energetically efficient than what we developed later on. This level of efficiency must have been

enough, however, since Lucy's species, called *Australopithecus afarensis*, existed for at least 900,000 years. She was certainly well adapted to the way she lived: some time spent in the trees, some on the ground. Her life was diverse, full of possibilities.

Even though 40 percent of Lucy's skeleton was recovered, controversies still exist when interpreting her life history. Some people even claim that she was not a young woman but a man, about forty years of age— a Lucifer rather than Lucy. But if scientists were polled, the majority would still see in these bones a young female with the pelvis of a woman.

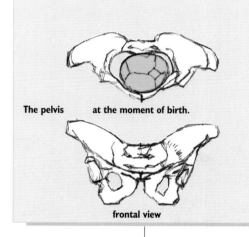

"MODERN LUCY" Lucy's pelvis tells us that it is not only human but also feminine. When compared with the male pelvis, it is wider, more open, with the lower portion of the spinal column and its fused vertebrae (the sacrum) more solid and broad. The majority of specialists believe that Lucy must have given birth to her children almost the way a modern woman does.

The pelvis   at the moment of birth.

frontal view

There are several re-creations of Lucy and her group. Some make her almost a woman, others give her the head of a chimpanzee. There are not enough pieces of the skull to make it possible to re-create her face with certainty. As for the hair, this, of course, remains an unknown.

How did we arrive at Lucy and family?
What happened four, five, or six million years ago?
What kind of primates were the first bipeds?

We continue to try to find out answers to these questions. In this quest, paleontologists have gone back to the Ethiopian Afar and to Kenya, hoping to discover what sort of beings lived in these regions before Lucy. They have focused their research in areas that provide more ancient sediments, and in doing so have found many interesting little fragments.

Climber or Biped?

First: pieces of skull, part of a jawbone, and the bones of a left arm. They belonged to a being that lived more than one million years before Lucy. Found in Ethiopia at a site called Aramis, south of the area in which the *Afarensis* lived, they are fascinating: Their characteristics are, like those of Lucy, extraordinarily mixed. Along with a baby tooth that greatly resembles that of a modern chimpanzee, this being had small canines, as did other hominids. Along with arm joints that are those of a real climber, the opening at the base of the skull, which connects to the spinal column, occupies a rather central position, implying a biped with upright posture. So what are we to conclude?

Ardipithecus

Lucy had characteristics of both a human and an ape. The fossil discovered in Aramis raises the possibility that we are seeing something between the ape and the *Australopithecus*. The balance tends toward the latter, but just barely. Finally, this small being (weighing approximately 66 lb. or 30 kg) was classified as a new genus: *Ardipithecus*. It is not an "australo" because of the truly primitive character of its teeth: Their very thin enamel is more like that of the fruit-eating great

There are many ways to move . . . but also specific ways, in different structures, of carrying the head and the pelvis.

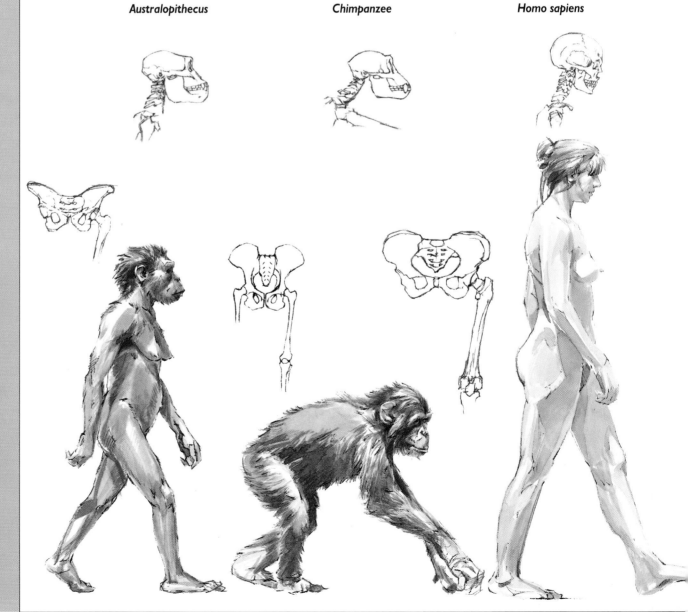

Australopithecus

Chimpanzee

Homo sapiens

UPRIGHT
ON EARTH

apes than that of hominids like us, who have thicker enamel. In this region of Africa thus lived, long before Lucy, another "small person," already a biped but bearing a greater resemblance than Lucy did to the great apes of its time.

Anamensis

Two to three hundred thousand years later, in the north of Kenya, there lived another species. Its remains were found near Lake Turkana and so were called australopithecus of the lake (or *anamensis:* "anam" means lake in the local language). It was also a biped, judging by its almost human tibia, and primitive, judging by its strong canines . . . . It probably weighed between 103 and 121 pounds (47–55 kg). Its discoverers put it in the same group as Lucy. Thus, these quasi-apes were already walking on two feet 4 to 5 million years ago.

Between Forests and Savannas

In what landscapes did these hominids evolve? That depends on which evidence you favor. It has often been said that if our unknown ancestors started to walk on their hind legs, it was because the forests in which they lived had become less dense. And since the savannas were increasing in size, they had to come down from the trees more often, to leave this protective shelter. However, the remains found with those of Aramis—forest monkeys and various seeds—indicate a wooded environment. On the other hand, those of Lake Turkana suggest an open environment with a large gallery forest: There were antelopes, baboons, hyenas . . . as well as fish and aquatic reptiles. Lucy seems to have lived in such an open environment. Apparently, many lifestyles were possible for bipeds. Not surprisingly, several species of bipeds probably lived at this time.

THE OLDEST HOMINID

Beyond 4 million years ago, field excavations have not provided much evidence. The Lothagam site, on the river west of Lake Turkana, has yielded several fragments of skull and an incomplete lower jawbone (mandible) that date from 5 to 5.5 million years ago. We believe that these were the remains of a hominid, perhaps an ancestor of later hominids, but can say nothing further. Unfortunately, great ape fossils of this period have not been found, so we are not able to go further back to our origins, toward the time when the two groups separated.

Where did they come from, where were they going? Three- and one-half million years ago, an adult and a "child" walked in the ashes of a recent volcanic eruption. This must have happened many times. And been erased almost as often. Except . . .

. . . except in Laetoli, in Tanzania, where these tracks from 35,000 centuries ago were preserved over a distance of twenty meters.

Four-million-year inquiry.

CAN THE BIRTH OF HUMANS BE TOLD?

Hundreds, perhaps thousands, of stories explain how humankind appeared on Earth. Many evoke a first man and a first woman created from parts by a god, by a natural force, by a divine animal.

What are scientists? Can they tell us a good story? Yes or no? What the scientific vision of origins can make us understand is that the characteristics of the human organism appeared progressively over the course of millions of years.

All of the Time That Was Needed

First, this vision tells us about periods of time that are difficult for us to imagine, then recounts changes for which we can understand neither the mechanisms nor the causes. In order for humans more or less like us to walk on their two feet on the surface of Earth, it was necessary that 2, 3, or 4 million years earlier, small beings performing acrobatics in the trees were also capable of walking upright properly on the ground. And it was necessary that other beings could live in trees and move from them by suspending themselves from branches 10 or 15 million years earlier still. Finally it was necessary that all the small beasts that do not resemble us begin simply to live and to run in the trees, 50 million years ago . . .

WHAT HUMANKIND?

More and more, what paleontologists are saying is that this history could have developed in a completely different manner. For 3 or 4 billion years, many chance events have occurred, such as the one that caused the extinction of dinosaurs. Without these events evolution would have taken an entirely different course. Climatic changes took place during the Tertiary period that necessarily shaped the course of events.

What can also be seen is that there is not one single story—a privileged lineage with its resulting "elite." Rather, each period might be explained in many ways. Until approximately 2 million years ago, two kinds of humans and two kinds of australopithecines may have coexisted in eastern Africa . . . . Ultimately, we are still searching for the answer that explains the events that have led us down the evolutionary path to who we are today.

Numerous Scenarios

Thus, we can tell a story of sorts, but it is a story that contains few details. Here we see fossils that can evoke particular moments in an evolutionary process. It remains very difficult today, in this world of bones dispersed over more than 70 million years, to determine who is descended from whom. As soon as we try to be more precise, disagreements arise. At least four outlines, four hypotheses exist that attempt to explain the genealogy of the first humans. As new discoveries are made, these outlines must frequently be modified.

Orangutan

Who Are We?

From which australopithecines are humans descended? Were they born at the same time as these "australos"? Did another type of australopithecine live between it and us? Are we descended from beings like Lucy, or did humans already exist during her period? And we ourselves, from whom are we descended, from what early human being? Could there perhaps have been at least two of them, way back then? For the moment, no one can tell this story. All that can be said is that several groups of australopithecines existed, of which two (the "gracile" and the "robust") were, for a long moment, the contemporaries of humans. This branching out is in itself a revolution: Before, there was an imaginary "lineage," a linear succession of forms. What we can say, then, is that humans were far from being alone.

To explain the birth of humans, each civilization has its tale.

Proconsul

Gorilla

Chimpanzee

Human

Australopithecus

Sivapithecus

From the first hominoids to modern forms: the great tree of evolutionary events about which we are still far from knowing all the details.

Everything came from the forest. It was in this environment that primates were born and in which they evolved during the majority of their history. Then the savanna expanded . . .

BY THE LIGHT
OF CHROMOSOMES

In a photograph, chromosomes resemble strands of yarn, those small unusable ends that grandmothers keep in the bottom of the drawer, no one knows why.

Chromosomes, obviously, are not strands of yarn and are not found in old drawers. And they cannot be considered useless: Present in all of our cells, they are the carriers of genes, that is, several billion bits of coded information that direct the formation and the functioning of living beings.

$2 \times 23 = 46$ Strands

We have them, as does every other living being. Generally speaking, it can be said that each living species (or each group of species) retains its small package of its own strands. We humans possess forty-six strands: forty-six chromosomes of which twenty-three come from our mother and twenty-three from our father. Among our primate cousins, some have twenty, some have eighty-four . . .

Each Has Its Own

It is possible not only to count these chromosomes but also to observe their structure and, specifically, to see the positioning of the genes from which they are made. They differ from each other in their form and the position of these genes, which is how they can be distinguished. Each and every living species has its own set of chromosomes, called its "karyotype," formed by specific strands.

Where the Small Strands Show Their Differences

Just as paleontologists compare the shapes of beings, their skeletons, and their teeth, and thus identify their relatives, cytologists (specialists in living cells) compare the karyotypes of various groups. They find resemblances that are also signs of kinship. The karyotypes of humans and of great apes are very similar; for example, chromosome 6 is the same for us, for chimpanzees, and for gorillas. Does kinship mean that we have a common ancestor?

Look for the Ancestor

The strands behave in a strange way. They change themselves. In fact, rather than compare them to strands of yarn, think of them as minuscule electronic devices. Click: They reverse themselves. Click: They join. Click: Only half of the strand reverses itself and the other joins another strand. Click: They divide in half . . . . The game—if this can be called a game, since in reality it involves lengthy research—consists of identifying each difference and, when there are two karyotypes that are very similar, looking for their common ancestor and suggesting the changes, the mutations, the "clicks" that made it possible to pass from the ancestral karyotype to the two current forms, similar but different.

Cercopithecus

Spider monkeys

Woolly monkeys

Right monkeys

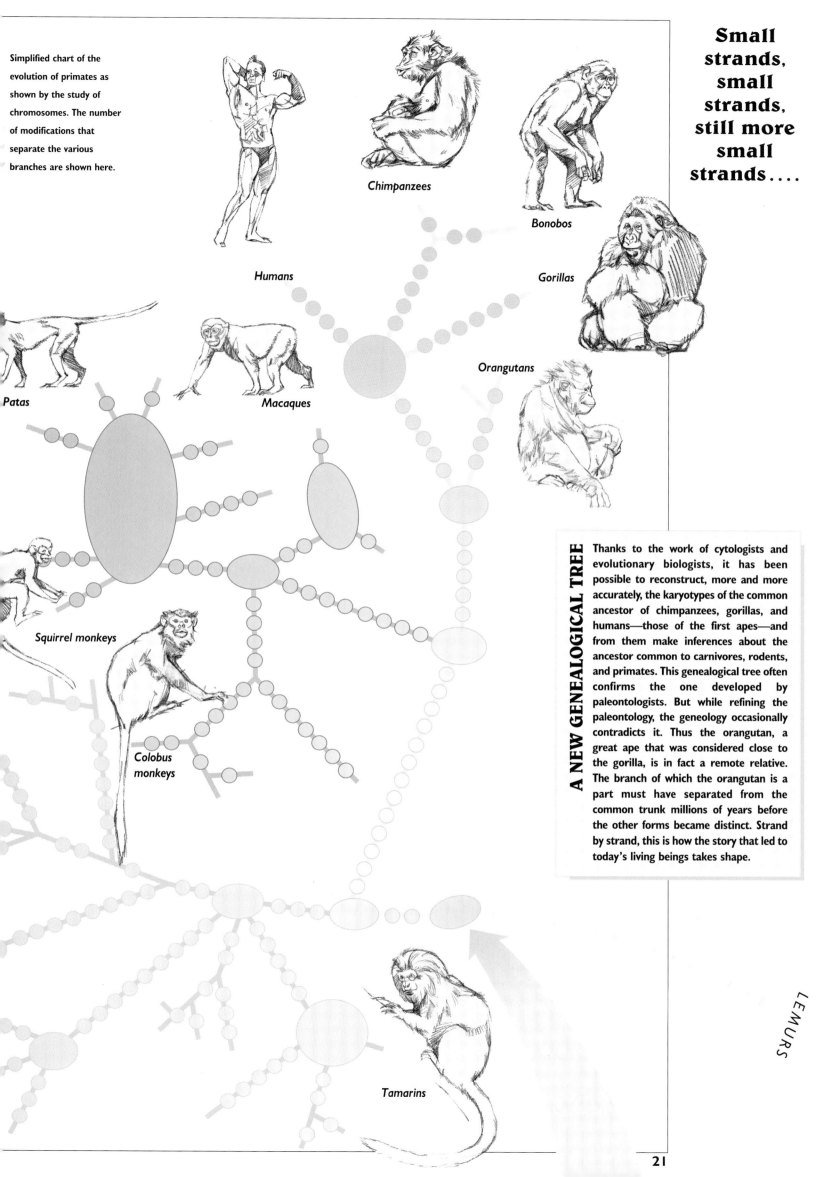

Simplified chart of the evolution of primates as shown by the study of chromosomes. The number of modifications that separate the various branches are shown here.

Humans

Chimpanzees

Bonobos

Gorillas

Orangutans

Patas

Macaques

Squirrel monkeys

Colobus monkeys

A NEW GENEALOGICAL TREE

Thanks to the work of cytologists and evolutionary biologists, it has been possible to reconstruct, more and more accurately, the karyotypes of the common ancestor of chimpanzees, gorillas, and humans—those of the first apes—and from them make inferences about the ancestor common to carnivores, rodents, and primates. This genealogical tree often confirms the one developed by paleontologists. But while refining the paleontology, the geneology occasionally contradicts it. Thus the orangutan, a great ape that was considered close to the gorilla, is in fact a remote relative. The branch of which the orangutan is a part must have separated from the common trunk millions of years before the other forms became distinct. Strand by strand, this is how the story that led to today's living beings takes shape.

Tamarins

LEMURS

THE ENVIRONMENT **OF EARLY HUMANS**

Today, Lucy's landscape is like a desert and extremely hot. But 3 million years ago, the bottom of an Ethiopian rift was a lake. It existed for tens of thousands of years.

Numerous ephemeral streams and rivers poured in. Surrounding the lake were swamps, some forests, and savannas dotted with bushes and acacia trees. Depending on the variations in climate, a mountain-style forest might have stretched out nearby.

The Time of the Animals

Animals were abundant, with a diversity that, even in Africa, is no longer encountered. It was possible to see the ancestors of elephants and also some of their now-extinct cousins, like the *Dinotheriums*. The ancestors of all modern African beasts and some others that are now extinct also lived there, such as the saber-toothed tiger (*Homotheriums*). The ancestors of horses were there, the small hipparions with three toes on each foot—a main hoof and two secondary hooves. There were gazelles, antelopes . . . particularly a specific group of antelopes, the impalas, found today in wooded savannas, which gives us an idea of the countryside at that time. The temperature was rather nice: 64.4–68°F (18–20°C) in January, 88–97°F (31–36°C) in July. Annual rainfall was from 200 to 320 inches (500–800 mm). All of this is known based on the remains of plants, most often from fossilized pollens, from the temperatures and the rain that they required.

The Formation of the Savannas

But the world changed. In the east, the two rifts, the large fractures in Earth's crust, expanded and deepened from the beginning of the Pliocene epoch (5 million years ago). On either side of these gaps, the ground rose and high plateaus were formed. The raising of the plateaus and volcanoes then blocked the clouds and rain coming from the Atlantic, that until then had encountered no obstacles. Thus, both sides of the fracture changed greatly. In the west, the humid influences of the Gulf of Guinea continued to be felt and the large tropical and equatorial forest was maintained. But the clouds and the rain they brought could barely reach the east, where the climate became more arid, no longer receiving the rains or the monsoons from the Indian Ocean. This is how the savannas were formed, wooded or not, and the landscape was created.

The Incursion of Australopithecines

Into all of these savannas ventured some of the small beings that had been living in the trees. It was long believed that in the forest lands they did not have the resources the savannas offered.

Mr. and Mrs. *Australopithecus afarensis*, their children, and some relatives are pleased to invite you to their home in the acacia on the right when entering the small forest. There they are well protected from leopards and have a view of the volcano and the *Dinotheriums* that pass by.

Homotherium

Hipparion

Dinotherium

The situation, however, was more complex. Some australopithecines appear to have lived in wooded environments. Yet the fossil evidence from Chad showed that these beings could have flourished not only to the east of the Rift but also far to the west. Perhaps, then, our brave australopithecines lived throughout a belt of wooded savannas and mixed, varied landscapes that must have bordered the great African forest; they lived in the east, probably, but also to the north and to the west.

Three million years ago, the fauna of eastern Africa included animals that are now extinct, including the impressive *Homotherium* with its enormous upper canines (it was said that they made it possible for it to pierce the thick skin of elephants); *Hipparion*, a predecessor of the horse; and *Dinotherium*, whose tusks, unlike modern elephants, curved not upward but downward.

Three million years ago, Africa was different.

The males were very gorilla-like, with their ridges on top of the skull and on the neck. From the beginning, this robust australopithecine (as it is sometimes called) was viewed as a being that was destined to be swept aside rather quickly.

PARADOXICAL PARANTHROPUS

There it is: These "paranthropines" did not exist when Lucy did. They were born after forms that appear more "advanced" than they are and they flourished at the same time as the first humans; and they lasted, in all, perhaps one-and-a-half million years. Who were these strange beings who seem to defy the solidly established principles of succession?

Double Response to Change

There are several forms of robust australopithecines. The oldest known example (again a female) was found in the Lake Turkana region, in Kenya. She is 2.6 million years old. Another type existed in Tanzania, in Olduvai, approximately 1.8 million years ago, a third in South Africa somewhat later. During this time the climate cooled markedly, aridity increased, and, as a result, the savannas expanded. At this moment there appeared—almost at the same time, let us say—both humans and these paranthropines. It is difficult not to see in this a double response to these changes: an increase in brain size and a massive jaw with large, solid teeth.

Solid Teeth

Paranthropines were sturdily built! Bipeds, obviously, but still capable of climbing in trees, they were particularly notable for their gigantic teeth and their ability to grind hard food when eating. Not only were their teeth impressive because of their size, they also had very thick enamel. Clearly they were designed to chew hard things, an idea reinforced by the powerful muscular connections of the jaws. These beings must have eaten tough food. This is understandable: The savanna does not contain the tender food of the forest. There are grains, dry fruit protected by hard skins, roots, all items that require a certain amount of effort, particularly to chew. Paranthropines' teeth were often very worn.

Not So Dumb!

These were not idiots. If we look at the volume of their cranium, which reveals the size of the brain, we find the same capacity as that of a gorilla. The latter, however, is four times larger than a paranthropine. In addition, it is possible that these powerful masticators would also have been able to use tools: Some sites in South Africa that have yielded the remains of paranthropines also contained sticks for digging. Their hands appear as dextrous as those of humans, their contemporaries.

An Efficient System

In any event, the paranthropine system was efficient: This group is, among all the hominids of that time, including *Homo*, the one for which we have the most fossils. Thus for a long time, it seems to have been the most successful—which should make us modest.

The two forms of hominids that were the contemporaries of the first humans: top, *Australopithecus africanus* (or the "gracile" form); bottom, *Paranthropus robustus*. This is the "robust" form that was the second to appear, at approximately the same time as humans.

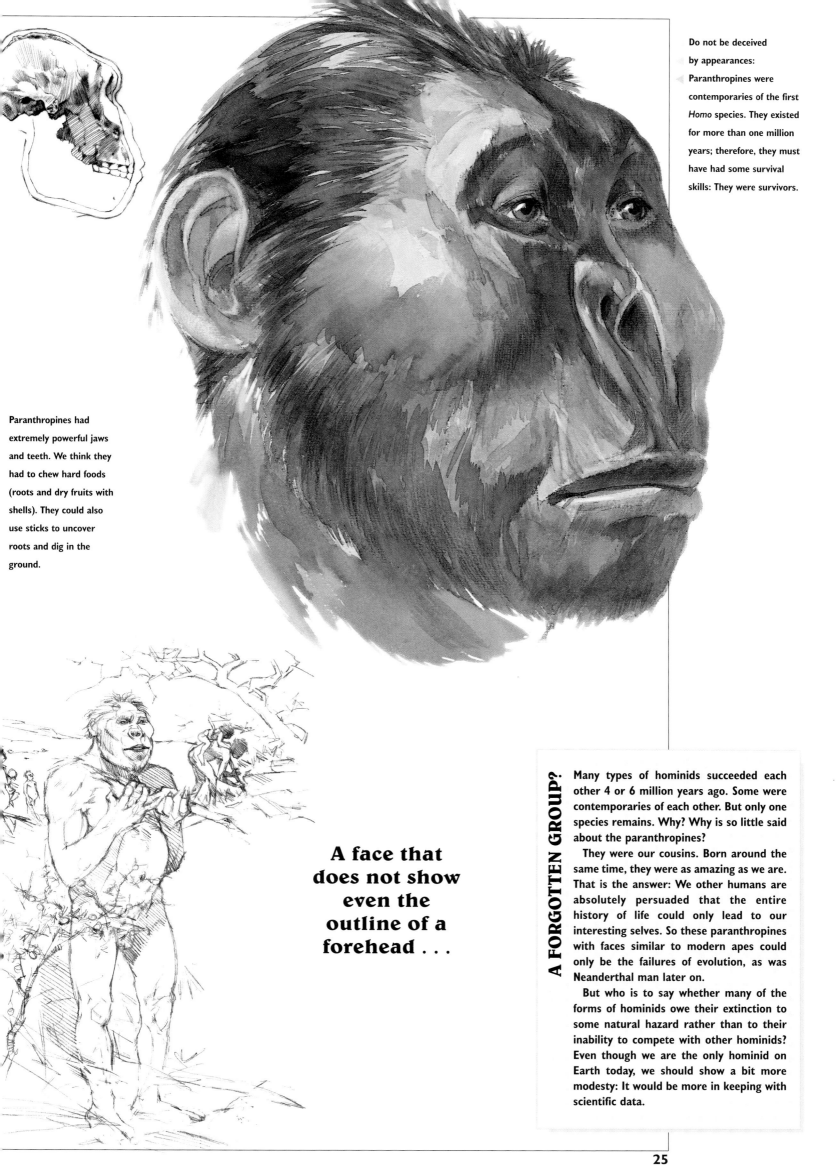

Paranthropines had extremely powerful jaws and teeth. We think they had to chew hard foods (roots and dry fruits with shells). They could also use sticks to uncover roots and dig in the ground.

A face that does not show even the outline of a forehead . . .

A FORGOTTEN GROUP?

Many types of hominids succeeded each other 4 or 6 million years ago. Some were contemporaries of each other. But only one species remains. Why? Why is so little said about the paranthropines?

They were our cousins. Born around the same time, they were as amazing as we are. That is the answer: We other humans are absolutely persuaded that the entire history of life could only lead to our interesting selves. So these paranthropines with faces similar to modern apes could only be the failures of evolution, as was Neanderthal man later on.

But who is to say whether many of the forms of hominids owe their extinction to some natural hazard rather than to their inability to compete with other hominids? Even though we are the only hominid on Earth today, we should show a bit more modesty: It would be more in keeping with scientific data.

HOMO HERE, HOMO THERE

Elongated or shortened faces, powerful or less powerful jaws, smaller or larger brains, heavy or light skeletons: We find all of them in the galleries of human origins.

So many beings that resembled humans more than apes were appearing in our fossil records. There was the *Ardipithecus*, the australopithecines, which were very diverse, and finally the strange group of paranthropines. It seems that all possible combinations were tried. Throughout the extended beginnings of bipedal beings, there was a real abundance of types, to which humans would soon be added.

Homo habilis

Paleontologists first presented us with *Homo habilis* during the 1960s: A hominid who lived in Olduvai in Tanzania appeared to be much handier than the australopithecines. *Homo habilis* was the first hominid to appear who greatly resembled us, one with lighter jaws, a larger brain (46 cu. in. or 750 cm^3), and the ability to make stone tools. *Homo habilis* entered the scene approximately 1.8 million years ago. Not long after, another hominid appeared in the fossil record— *Homo erectus*, who was next in line.

Homo erectus

These hominids were very successful at making stone tools, especially bifaces. They were bigger, apparently more intelligent (with a brain as large as 61 cubic inches or 1000 cm^3 or more), and seemed to establish themselves quickly. That they appeared 1.7 million years ago meant that there was no longer much room for *Homo habilis*. However, this *Homo habilis* had his predecessors, and even competitors.

Homo rudolfensis

A beautiful fossil was found in the north of Kenya, in Koobi Fora near Lake Turkana (then called Lake Rudolf). It was first described as *Homo habilis* (1.9 million years old). A later re-evaluation showed that it was another kind of hominid with an astonishing mixture of characteristics. For instance, it possessed a well-developed skull (close to 49 cubic inches, or 800 cm^3) with a high forehead, but had face and jaws like a paranthropine. A second fossil, a jawbone found in Malawi, was placed in the same group. At 2.4 million years of age this other *Homo rudolfensis* is the oldest

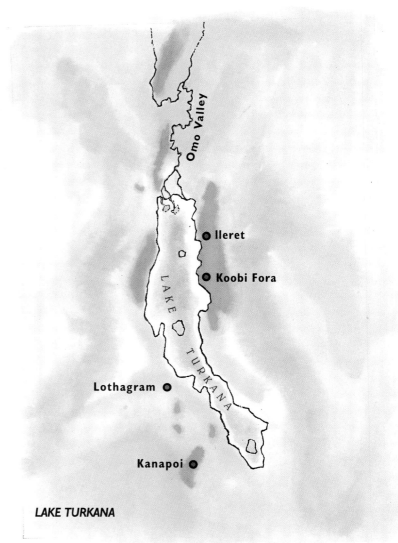

LAKE TURKANA

known human fossil.

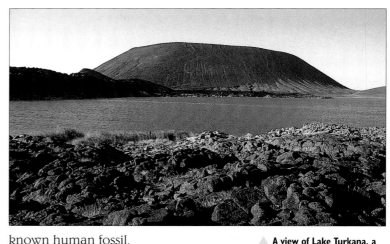

▲ A view of Lake Turkana, a vast depression of 3,320 square miles (8600 km²).

Homo ergaster

Still uncertain is whether another fossil from the same area, called *Homo ergaster*, was a unique species or a kind of *Homo erectus*. Whichever it is, it is another sign that there were many kinds of humans in a very short period of time. Did this very rapid succession represent diverse and varied trials, or was it coexistence?

Near the northern borders of Kenya, the Turkana region contains numerous sedimentary foundations rich in fossils from 1 to 3 million years old: a source of extraordinary discoveries about our origins.

Mr. *Homo habilis,* in an attempted re-creation based on known fossils. The naming of human fossils is subject to variations. The oldest were first all called *Homo habilis.* Today the tendency is to divide this group into *Homo rudolfensis* and *Homo habilis.*

Were there two early Homo species?

This skull found in Koobi Fora (Kenya) is 1,900,000 years old; it is the oldest known human skull, reconstructed based on 150 fragments. Rather rounded, it has an obviously human-like braincase, yet, unlike humans, it has a very powerful and heavy jawbone.

A BEAUTIFUL MOSAIC

And what if not one but two "first humans" had existed? It is curious that one of the two known types around 2 million years ago (*Homo habilis*) had very human-like jawbones, but retained some australopithecine characteristics in its limbs: Perhaps he still climbed trees . . . . And the other (*Homo rudolfensis*), in contrast, had very human limbs and a very ape-like jaw. The diversity went beyond this. Perhaps these two humans rubbed shoulders with two forms of australopithecines. One would be the robust form, the other a species with gracile jawbones. And all these people, humans or near-humans, walked on two feet, using their hands better than had the apes. Some climbed trees and the others did not. It was a strange world and a beautiful mosaic of solutions proposed for the future.

1 Hadar
2 Omo
3 Lokalelei
4 Olduvai

THOSE DREADFUL
FIRST TOOLS

One decisive criteria for recognizing humanity is the advent of stone tools, the sole remaining implements of early humans since the disappearance of the forest.

I t was first believed that the presence of stone tools in the fossil record marked an important threshold for humankind. The truth is, however, that we don't know who made the earliest stone tools. There were cut stones at Olduvai, first attributed to the paranthropine, discovered at the same level. Then a *Homo habilis* was uncovered in the same layers: Obviously, the making of the stones was attributed to him—and just like that, the paranthropine became inferior. Since then, other discoveries have put the birth of tools further back in time. And opinion has changed with these discoveries.

At the Dawn of the Tool

The Gona deposits in northeast Ethiopia, near the Hadar deposits, which contained Lucy and the *Afarensis* "family," produced stones clearly bearing traces of being knapped. The "Kada Gona EG 10 and EG 12" sites yielded almost 3,000 stone artifacts. Most are flakes that were broken—or knapped—from small cobbles. Dating was difficult but the sites were finally determined to be somewhere between 2.5 and 2.6 million years old. Currently, these are the oldest known tools.

In the Omo River

In southwest Ethiopia, large deposits from the Omo River also revealed interesting objects, dated from 2.34 to 2.35 million years ago. These objects were fragments knapped from small stones or nuggets of quartz. Attempts had obviously been made to shape the small stones, but not always with the greatest success. Most archaeologists agree with this assessment: Crushing was more common than real knapping.

Lokalelei

Finally, in the Lake Turkana region, the Lokalelei site also provided approximately five hundred of these more or less worked stone objects. These included flakes, generally broken, and the cores from which they had been knapped. The

Mrs. *Homo habilis* needed something to cut a branch. She had taken stones from the reserve or from the deposit or from the stream and had hit them against one another several times as she had been taught. From this she produced a flake with a sharp edge.

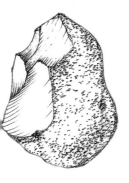

traces of removal suggested that here, too, the work had not been easy. Many mistakes and experiments took place 2.35 million years ago, when the beings whose identity we do not even know tried to chip away at these blocks.

Clumsy Pioneers

Here then are what must be called the first tools, even if they show many signs of breaking and failed blows—more failure, in fact, than success. Specialists speak of the "poor quality of worked material." These first artisans clearly were far from technical mastery! That they were not skilled toolmakers had nothing to do with these hominids being australopithecines. Why not? It has not been possible to establish any link between these worked stones and any particular human fossil. We have only the clear impression that 2.3 to 2.6 million years ago "something" was in the process of beginning. Who, then, was responsible for inventing the stone tool?

The cut stones of Gona are approximately 2,600,000 years old. These are the oldest known examples and consist of simple flakes and cobbles rather than carefully crafted tools.

There were many mistakes, 2.35 million years ago . . .

AT THE OLDUVAI SITE

After the rough shapes and the awkwardness, another 400,000 years passed without further visible progress. Nothing has yet been found from that interval. Then other worked objects appeared. Beginning 1.9 million years ago, the cut stones of Olduvai truly merit the name tools. They are deliberate enough so that paleontologists can study the way in which pieces were removed. Half of them showed an order, a logic. For example, the toolmaker had alternated, chipping one side and then the other. This represented a threshold that had been crossed. The tools had even begun to be differentiated: Some had taken the form of balls, others that of axes.

We were little: 4.5 feet (1.40 m) for the men, even less for the women, who must have weighed no more than 55 to 66 pounds (25–30 kg).

TO BE HUMAN IN THOSE TIMES

We now have a handsome head without much of a forehead (not at all similar to the wall that today sits above our eyebrows), a harmoniously inclined face (not a bizarre vertical face) and, finally, powerful and strongly muscled jaws, as were needed.

Set of Hands

Our hands were not very different from those of humans today. Some of us apparently still had a foot structure poorly adapted for walking and joints that still made it possible to climb in trees almost like monkeys . . . .We will not comment on this point. In any event, our hands were more agile—for grasping, waving, throwing, aiming, cutting, and shaping, as well as for caressing . . . and hitting.

Were We Hairy?

Serious question! Had the major process of hair disappearance already begun? We probably had more hair than the humans who came later—fortunately! But it is possible that we had already begun to distinguish ourselves from other animals in this area also.

Learning to Share

In any event, be assured that we lived well. If not, we would not have had these interesting descendants, and you would not be there to ask a thousand questions about us. We had what we needed: grasses, roots, fruits . . . and some carcasses, from time to time, delicious carrion that we were able to grab from nasty creatures. If we were able to live this well, it is obviously because we stayed together, in groups. We had what you call a social life. We helped each other, we shared . . . . We hugged each other, we groomed each other (don't you?). We also fought, obviously.

DID WE TALK?

Specialists have offered many theories on this subject. Some believe that language must not have appeared until very late in human evolution—in fact not until the appearance of *Homo sapiens*. Others think, based on the conformation of our mandibles and the base of our skulls (where the organs for speech are located) that at least a kind of language must have existed. Anthropologists maintain that the areas in the brain that control technical manipulation—like the cutting of tools—are closely related to those used in language and that, as a result, we, the first humans, must have had words, a language on the level of our basic technical skills. They are very kind . . . . But who knows whether, already, we knew how to tell stories? Isn't that the true essence of humans?

Long Live the Community

In short, we, the first humans, strongly suggest to you, the most recent on the scene, that you stop thinking of us as short, hairy, grunting brutes leading the life of hunted animals. This is completely improper, uncalled for, and totally unrealistic. A word to the wise is sufficient!

Tell yourselves that we were completely successful: Your own existence is the proof. And above all, men or women, we were beautiful, seductive, often happy with life. At least as much as you!

Here they are, in their daily life, our early humans! Of course, this is just supposition. All we have of these people is a few bones and some cut stones. We assume that they sat down or squatted, that they ate carrying their food to their mouths, that they spoke to each other, more or less, that they rested. They were at the beginning of a little of everything.

Although vast, our African birthplace nevertheless had its limits. And the rest of the world? When were the other continents populated, specifically Asia and Europe? And by whom?

Here we are faced with the problem of a more recent ancestor. First discovered in Java, in Indonesia, at the end of the last century and called *Pithecanthropus erectus*, then found in China and called *Sinanthropus*, then in northern Africa and in eastern Africa—all were finally admitted into the great chain of humanity: *Homo erectus*.

Conquering the World

The *Homo erectus* (standing men) of Africa were very different people from their predecessors. They were rather tall. In Kenya, in Nariokotome, a magnificent skeleton of a young adolescent (perhaps thirteen years old) was found that measured 5.4 feet (1.65 m). This was 1.5 million years before us . . . . *Homo erectus*, moreover, had a larger brain: around 61

cubic inches (1,000 cm^3) at the beginning and then increasing in size. If we were to run into one on the street, we would probably turn around, startled by the strong jaws, heavy and rounded chin, and the impressive bony ridge above the eyes . . . . But they had mastered excellent techniques for cutting, much more advanced than those of their predecessors. Seeing them this tall, strong, and capable, it seems natural that they were the first to leave Africa and travel elsewhere in the world.

1,800,000 Years Everywhere?

This is an ongoing controversy. With new dating techniques, some of the Java fossils were dated at 1.8 million years—almost the

The various routes that humans could have followed when they began to leave Africa. The sites are those described in the text, along with the oldest known sites in Eurasia.

Our origins? They took place in an immense theater—on the scale of a continent.

The Nariokotome adolescent (1.5 million years old) compared with a young, modern Caucasian boy of the same age (12–13).

OUT OF AFRICA

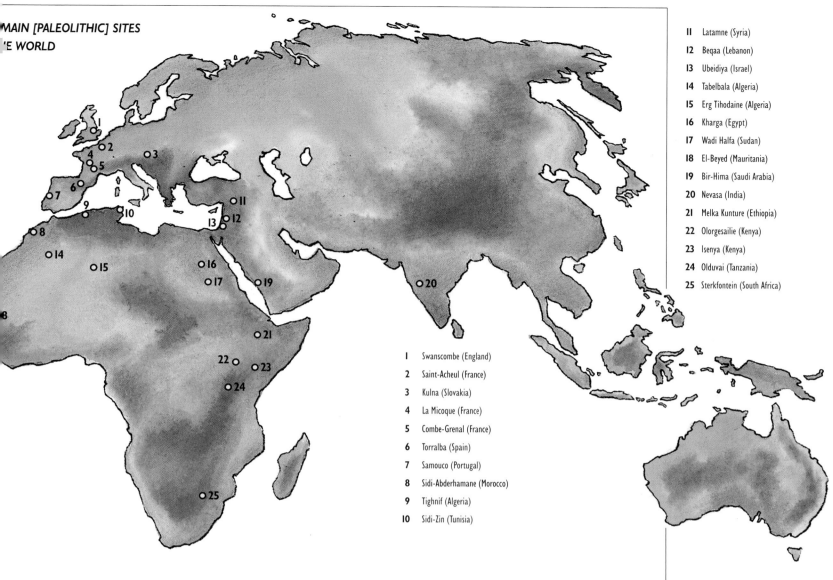

11 Latamne (Syria)

12 Beqaa (Lebanon)

13 Ubeidiya (Israel)

14 Tabelbala (Algeria)

15 Erg Tihodaine (Algeria)

16 Kharga (Egypt)

17 Wadi Halfa (Sudan)

18 El-Beyed (Mauritania)

19 Bir-Hima (Saudi Arabia)

20 Nevasa (India)

21 Melka Kunture (Ethiopia)

22 Olorgesailie (Kenya)

23 Isenya (Kenya)

24 Olduvai (Tanzania)

25 Sterkfontein (South Africa)

1 Swanscombe (England)

2 Saint-Acheul (France)

3 Kulna (Slovakia)

4 La Micoque (France)

5 Combe-Grenal (France)

6 Torralba (Spain)

7 Samouco (Portugal)

8 Sidi-Abderhamane (Morocco)

9 Tighnif (Algeria)

10 Sidi-Zin (Tunisia)

also discoveries in the south of Spain, in Auvergne . . . . Say no more!

Back to Square One

After a period of enthusiasm, the excitement began to ebb. The dates from the Caucasus, China, and Java appear problematic. The Spanish site is not as it was described . . . . Finally, in Africa a type was found that was first considered intermediate between *Homo habilis* and *Homo erectus* that would have been more than 2 million years old. Its cranial volume was the same as that of *Homo habilis*. It was classified as a distinct species: *Homo ergaster*, which may have simply been the oldest *Homo erectus*.

3,100 Miles in 100,000 Years

After all, was it such an accomplishment to reach Europe and the Orient from Africa? To cover 3,100 miles (5,000 km) in 100,000 years—a very short period in terms of ancient prehistory—it would have been enough to move 55 yards (50 m) further each year! No need to speak of conquest. In this way, it was possible to reach the ends of the earth practically without being aware of it—by advancing .6 mile (1 km) each generation.

same as in Africa! In China, the Longgupo site provided a tooth (only one!) and a piece of jawbone (no more) that may go back 1.8 to 1.9 million years. Finally, at the doors of Europe, a jawbone discovered in Dmanisi, in Georgia, and apparently primitive, was also dated at 1.8 million years. There were

THE HUMANS OF JAVA

It was in Java in 1890 that the *erectus* were first discovered. Theoreticians of Darwinism (evolution of species) had predicted the existence of an "anthropopithecus," that is, an intermediate being between humans and monkeys. A young Dutch doctor, Eugene Dubois, left for Java to begin his research. He actually found fossils (skull, limbs). Influenced by the ideas then in fashion, he called these fossils "pithecanthropus" (ape-men). However, they came from a being more human than ape, with a completely human brain and human skills. Subsequent discoveries were made in Java, some of the same type, others of more recent types. Establishing dates for these remains, however, is difficult; the terrain at the famous Indonesian deposits—Trinil, Sangiran, Modjokerto, Solo, Ngandong, Sambungmachan—has very uneven layers.

Europe is far when you come from Africa and you do not have a boat! It is far and, except on the shores of the Mediterranean, it is not always very warm. We know that this small end of Eurasia was late in being populated.

THE FIRST EUROPEANS

The first Europeans were
certainly *Homo erectus*.
Based on the known
fossils of this type of
human, here is how one
of these men might have
looked. The model was
made using processes
for reconstruction of
flesh used in
anthropology.

PIONEERS OR PARIAHS?

Humans were not really in a hurry to "conquer" Europe, if we believe the most reasonable of recent estimates. Let us accept that they were present in Italy, Spain, and France some 1 million years ago. The Ubeidiya archaeological record, in Israel, was dated to 1.4 million years; therefore, a minimum of 300,000 years were needed to cover 1,860 miles (3,000 km). That means they traveled .6 mile (1 km) every three centuries. Was Europe that unattractive?

The worked stones present with the fossils are also astonishing. They are between 800,000 and 900,000 years old, and are the only such tools found at these European sites—for the moment, of course. But this represents a considerable technical delay (1 million years) compared to Africa. And so we ask ourselves whether, far from being hardy pioneers, the first Europeans might instead have been marginal types, who arrived in these rather inhospitable regions because the competition was too strong elsewhere—outcasts, in a word.

For many years, the oldest known human remains in Europe consisted of a powerful jawbone found in 1907 in the south of Germany, near Heidelberg, the jawbone known as the "Mauer," estimated to be 500,000 or 600,000 years old. This is a real youngster, compared with the first fossils from Africa and even Asia.

And Why Not Us?

Then European researchers seemed to challenge this sequence, as if to say, "And why not us?" Names of sites were circulated, along with exciting numbers. In France first, with sites in the Auvergne: First 900,000, then 1,800,000 years were mentioned; then in Spain, with similar dates; in Italy . . . . The discovery of another very powerful jawbone in Georgia, in Dmanisi confirmed these ages: This fossil came from a *Homo erectus* 1,800,000 years old. Although Georgia is not officially part of Europe, it is close, and it is certainly one of the roads that lead there. From Georgia, following, perhaps, the shores of the Black Sea, it would have been possible to reach the Russian steppes and, by so doing, to become the first Europeans . . .

Disaster

These fossils suggested our ancestors had lived in Georgia 1.8 million years ago, the same in the Auvergne and in the south of Spain (in Orce). At the same time, sites 2 million years old or more were mentioned: almost like Africa! But in science, as elsewhere, we must beware of wishful thinking. Re-examined, the fossils, the dating, and the sites didn't hold up. Thus, new tests showed the Dmanisi jawbone as more recent, Neanderthal, in fact, a descendent of *Homo erectus.* The sites in the Auvergne seemed more difficult to place in time. And the age of the Orce site also proved wrong.

Investigation at 800,000 Years

Did this mean we had to go back to our meager 500,000 years? Not quite. In Auvergne, one site remains: Soleihac. Investigators have not found human fossils there but mainly stone tools that are about 970,000 years old, according to dating by volcanic rock. In central Italy, the Ceprano calotte, which turned up in a trench by a highway, is between 700,000 and 800,000 years old. Finally, in Spain, the Sierra of Atapuerca is the great European revelation of recent times. One of the sites, the "Gran Dolina," produced fragments of bone, human teeth, and cut stone that dated back 800,000 years. The first European inhabitants then, apparently lived between 800,000 and 1 million years ago. Then, as investigations continued, the beginning of the 1990s brought new thinking . . .

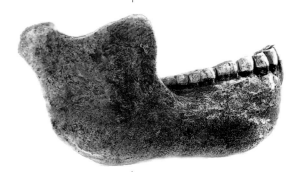

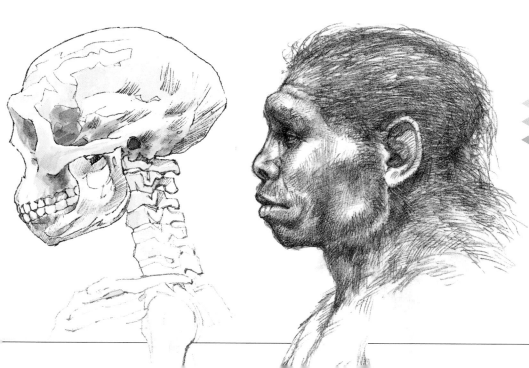

Europe is hard, hard, when you are accustomed to the African heat!

Not content with having been the most enduring of human types, Homo erectus also created the technology that certainly lasted longer than any other in our history.

STONE TOOLS, BIFACES, AND COMPANY

This technical culture, symbolized by the stone tool called the biface, began in Africa 1.7 million years ago and still existed on three continents (with the exception of the Far East) 200,000 or 300,000 years ago.

The Acheulean

The name of this culture comes from Saint-Acheul, a suburb of Amiens, in France. It was there, around 1860, that bifaces were identified and first placed in time.

The biface is a symmetrical tool with two faces, made from a stone that has, through successive chipping, been shaped like an almond. These tools suggest, first that our ancestors recognized a need for such a form and second, that it was possible to create it. In fact, the biface already requires considerable know-how. Prehistorians know how to make them and have discovered that, in order to cut them, it was necessary to use not other stones but materials that they call "tenders," such as hammers made from the antlers of stags.

Were They Gifted, Homo erectus?

The biface was not the only tool. Masses of small detached fragments of flint or other nodules were used (more or less well). In Isenya, in Kenya, 700,000 years ago, *Homo erectus* made "choppers" and "hand axes." In studying and reproducing how these choppers were shaped, investigators discovered that these pieces occasionally demonstrated a type of genius: Some of them were formed using only two blows, including cutting! Of course, this elegant economy was possible only by choosing the most suitable form from the outset. But knowing how to make these decisive blows was still necessary.

An Enigma to Be Solved

In fact, although we can imagine the use of a chopper and hand axe, no one can say what these people did with their bifaces. Making such an object required some time. And for what purpose? They are not very convenient weapons. They might be used to pierce or cut . . . but

▲ Seen from the front and
▲ side, an acheulean biface
▲ 6.5 inches (17 cm) long.

points and sharp edges can be obtained in a much more simple and economical fashion. So? Some have called them objects of prestige. Certainly, these great acheuleans continue to amaze us.

BOUCHER DE PERTHES

The discovery of the bifaces marked the birth of prehistoric science in the nineteenth century. In the 1830s, these first stone tools had been found in Picardy, France. Fascinated by this subject, a customs inspector from Abbeville, Jacques Boucher de Crèvecoeur de Perthes (1788–1868), explored the region. He found many other stone tools under many layers of earth and at the same level as the bones of such extinct animals as the mammoth. For him, this was evidence that humans had lived earlier than had been thought. But few people believed him, and French scientists initially refused to travel to examine the sites. It would take the visit of English geologists, particularly Hugh Falconer, for them finally to admit the great age of man and thus prehistory.

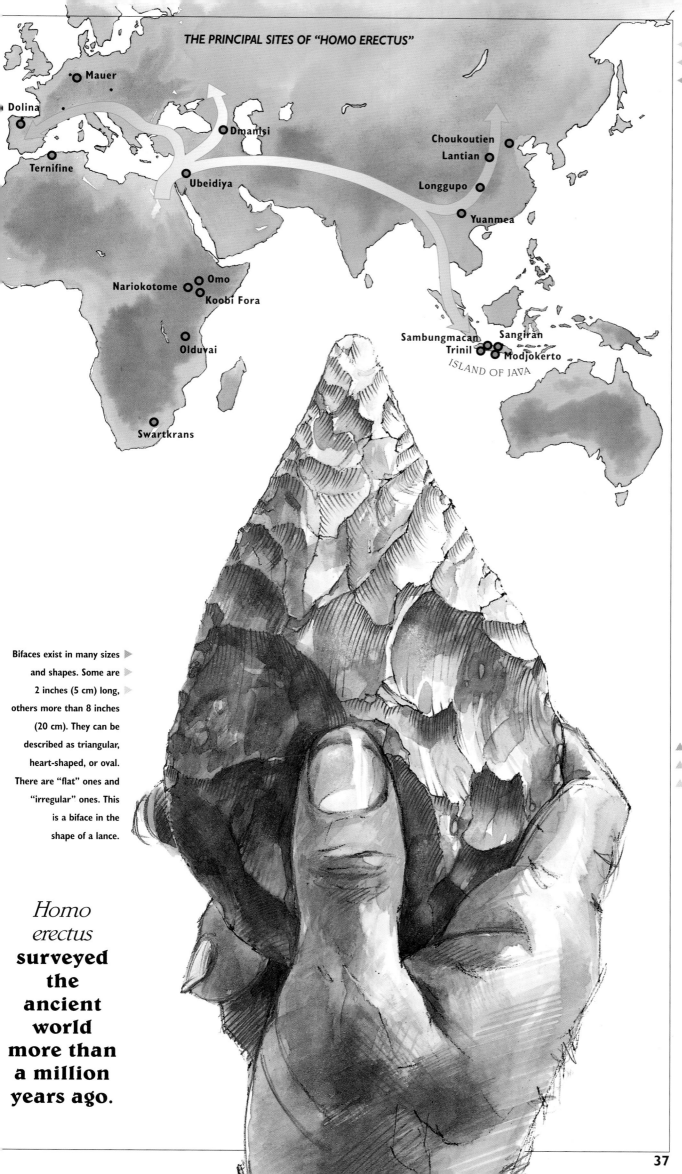

THE PRINCIPAL SITES OF "HOMO ERECTUS"

Mauer

Dolina

Ternifine

Dmanisi

Ubeidiya

Choukoutien
Lantian

Longgupo

Yuanmea

Nariokotome • Omo
Koobi Fora

Olduvai

Swartkrans

Sambungmacan • Sangiran
Trinil • Modjokerto
ISLAND OF JAVA

This map shows that the technique of the biface did not penetrate the Far East (with the exception of Japan and Korea). One possible explanation for this is the presence in this area of bamboo, from which it was possible to make very sharp cutting tools; stone was not necessary. And since bamboo does not last, prehistorians have no evidence of these tools, if they existed.

Archaelogists have learned how to make bifaces, which allows them to determine in what order the fragments were removed from fossils and even the mistakes made by the prehistoric "shaper."

Bifaces exist in many sizes and shapes. Some are 2 inches (5 cm) long, others more than 8 inches (20 cm). They can be described as triangular, heart-shaped, or oval. There are "flat" ones and "irregular" ones. This is a biface in the shape of a lance.

Homo erectus **surveyed the ancient world more than a million years ago.**

THE MIRACLE OF FIRE

That which keeps away predators and brings together men . . .

It is hard to believe that humans could have lived without fire for most of their history. Nevertheless, what happened to them is perhaps a good thing.

Humans lived without fire for perhaps one hundred thousand generations. Even today, Inuit who do not know about fire live in Canada, a cold climate. Ethnologists have gone to live with them and report that it is possible. The very early humans did not warm their hands around the fire in the evening.

But One Day . . .

When and how did this great discovery take place? No one can say. Traces of evidence were found in Africa suggesting that humans already knew about fire one million years ago or more. Archaeologists find these traces rather tenuous and unconvincing. They also do not place much stock in traces of fire found in a cave in Provence, near Durance, France, which may provide evidence of an intentional inferno 700,000 years ago. Is this true? How can the distinction be made between natural fires and those of humans? We will have to wait to find out.

With or Without a Fixed Home?

The cave of Mas des Caves in Languedoc, between Montpellier and Nimes, France, must have been an agreeable place to live at that time. There are remains of many fireplaces, with their stones and burnt areas, as well as devices intended to divert water from the stream that ran in the cave. These "pleasant moments around the fire" are dated at 400,000 years or a bit more. In Brittany, the Ménez Drégan site, a deposit that has experienced much erosion from the sea, has been dated to 465,000 years: There traces remain of calcination and assemblages of stones that call to mind the design of a fireplace.

THE RAW AND THE COOKED

Humans seem to have always tried to distinguish themselves from nonhumans. One of the ways they did so was to prepare, to transform food: to cook. Of course, fruits were always eaten, but cooked or boiled foods may be as old as fire itself. There are many ways in which to transform one's food. Meats or roots can be heated (or grilled) on burning stones. They can be placed under these stones, a technique tried in the South American Andes and in Europe probably 12,000 to 20,000 years ago. Finally, it is possible to heat water in a water skin (or in the stomach of an animal) by putting burning stones into it. By adding in bones, preferably those with marrow, excellent soups were made; and the well-known boiled dinners were created by adding pieces of meat. In any case, whatever recipes Paleolithic humans used, we must banish the idea that all they did was tear apart raw meat with their teeth.

Terra Amata

Thus fire was made in France 400,000 years ago. It was made on the shores of the Mediterranean, in Nice, approximately 380,000 years ago. The site consists of very old dunes, traces of a hut whose posts were held in place by stones, and finally some other stones arranged around a hole with calcinated ground. The site is called Terra Amata ("beloved earth").

Tending the Fire

It would be at approximately that time, between 350,000 and 500,000 years ago, that humans first tamed fire. How did they do it? We do not know. Did they know how to light this fire, or did they simply maintain it after they discovered a fire in the forest, for example? We do not know. What is certain, however, is that the most recent prehistoric sites have fireplaces and that, 15,000 years ago, our ancestors knew many ways to light a fire. Presumably, it all began with naturally occurring fires, brush fires, for example, or forest fires that, even today, begin spontaneously in very hot weather or by lightning strikes. Picking up a burning

The "Etruscan" rhinoceros and the "southern" elephant: two of the impressive animals alive at the time that humans domesticated fire.

branch, live charcoal, biting into "cooked" roots or "roasted" animals and finding that it is not bad may have contributed. And noting that all animals, even the largest, run away from fire . . .

The First Homes

And with fire came other changes. Humans began to create living areas, blocks of posts or arrangements of caves. Not only could they warm themselves, but they could take shelter. Perhaps they had already slept in caves and constructed huts, but there is no sure indication. It can only be said that, 400,000 years ago, in the country that would one day be called France, humans created homes in all senses of the word. With walls of stone or of wood, they separated themselves from the world. And they perhaps began to cook their food, which is certainly one of the most interesting ways of distinguishing themselves from nature and the animal world.

One of the oldest known fireplaces: that of Terra Amata, in France. It is modest, to be sure . . . but one has to start somewhere. Ethnology has made it possible to list a number of ways of lighting a fire without using either lighter or matches (not invented until 1827): the sparks that fall on flammable moss, the stick rotated very quickly in a hole that begins to smoke and redden when it is accelerated by a bow system. In recent prehistoric sites, some indications suggest that humans used such methods.

For the last two million years, climate fluctuations have become more pronounced. At the time when the last "erectus" lived, the cool periods had become really cold in Europe and Asia.

It was the time of the great glaciations.

EARTH, 130,000 YEARS AGO

In the history of Earth, periods of glaciation seem to arrive every 200 million years. Traces of them are visible in rocks dating back 600, 400, and 200 million years, on some rocks from the Paleozoic era in the Sahara, for example.

When the Sun Pales

It appears that the sun, in its journey all around the center of our galaxy (as the stars also rotate . . .), every 200 million years crosses a large zone in which the dust is thicker than elsewhere. This causes a bit less warmth for Earth—not much less, but enough to throw our climate out of balance. To this is added the small changes that take place in Earth's orbit, whose angle can also vary. The point at which Earth is the closest to the sun is called its perihelion. Over time, the perihelion has changed; these small changes involve minor changes in

SEA LEVELS

The volume of accumulated ice represented an enormous reduction in the water in the oceans and the atmosphere: Sea levels were significantly lower than today. They must have decreased to approximately –395 or –425 feet (–120 or –130 m). That means that a body of water such as the English Channel did not exist but had been replaced by a vast plain. A large portion of the North Sea also disappeared. Rivers such as the Loire and the Garonne had to travel an additional 62 to 93 miles (100–150 km) to reach the sea. The Rhine traveled to the English Channel or to Norway . . . . The Po ran to an Adriatic Sea reduced to a narrow gulf. In Asia, Java, Sumatra, and Borneo were part of the continent, Japan was connected to Korea, and, in the distant north, Siberia was connected to Alaska. At the same time, Australia and New Zealand were one. This also means that the increase in sea level must have drowned many prehistoric sites, particularly coastal sites, which were among the most interesting.

Modern Greenland makes ▶ it possible to imagine what the Alps or Scotland must have been like during the last glaciation.

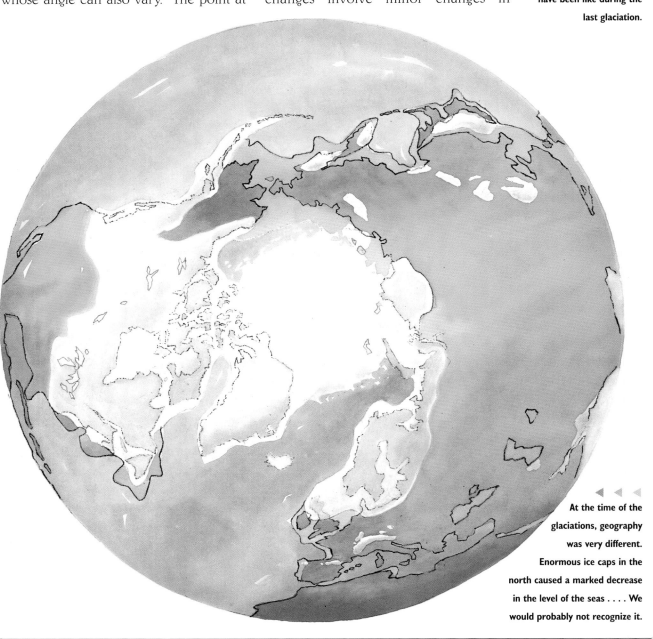

◀ ◀ ◀
At the time of the glaciations, geography was very different. Enormous ice caps in the north caused a marked decrease in the level of the seas . . . . We would probably not recognize it.

sunlight. And these small changes are enough to cause a glaciation or, by successive fluctuations, to make one vanish.

A Coat of Ice

A glaciation? This is, first of all, ice. Approximately 130,000 years ago, during the next-to-last period of glaciations, a coat of ice covered all of the Alps. More than glaciers, it was an ice sheet with glacial tongues 31 to 62 miles (50–100 km) long that reached as far as the plains. The Alpine ice sheet was so thick that it extended above the Jura mountains. The glaciers of the Pyrenees reached as far as the foot of the chain, as far as Lourdes, for example. The Carpathian glaciers were also long in reach. Even in Corsica traces have been found of glaciers and eternal snow.

An Antarctica in Europe

All of this was nothing in comparison with the gigantic ice sheets that covered all of the north and a large portion of northwest Europe. At its peak, the ice covered most of the British Isles and Ireland, most of the North Sea, the northern part of Germany, Poland, and Russia. Eliminated from the map were Scotland, Denmark, Norway, Sweden, the Baltic countries—and Switzerland, of course, drowned under the Alps. Across thousands of miles and thousands of feet of thickness, a formidable plateau of ice weighed down the north of the continent. Only the glacial expanses of Greenland and Antarctica give us an idea of what it was like. North America was affected in the same way as Europe, and perhaps a bit more. Glaciers reached as far as New York and created immense *lobes* in the plains of the Midwest.

Cold? Yes, but Not Always

As for temperatures, they were 6 to 8 degrees lower in the south of France when compared with today, 10 degrees or more in Belgium and in Central Europe. In summer, floating ice was seen in the Atlantic as far as the northern coast of Spain. The landscape was also profoundly different. But glaciation was not a permanent state: There were at least as many temperate episodes as there were episodes of cold. Thus the trees became more numerous, the ice floes moved away, and the level of the seas rose.

CLIMATIC FLUCTUATIONS DURING THE LAST 1.8 MILLION YEARS

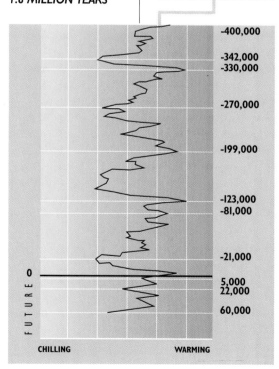

This diagram is based on a core of sediments taken from the bottom of the Pacific Ocean. It shows that the number of fluctuations was very great. It also shows (below) that the diagram is extended toward the future. Without the intervention of human activities, we would have the beginning of glaciation in 22,000 years and a great stroke of cold in 60,000 years.

Neanderthal

HELLO, MR. NEANDERTHAL

Allow us to introduce the Neanderthal family. Handsome, aren't they? And to think that for the longest time we considered them half-apes!

In 1856, in the Neander Valley, workers found the top of a skull that proved difficult to characterize. Was it from a "primitive" race of humans, or was it the remains of an abnormal being?

Only with the discovery of other fossils, specifically from Spy in Belgium, could this different ancient human form be included with modern man—the first to be so recognized.

Different from Us, That Is Sure

They are so different that at first the Neander remains were seen as intermediate between modern man and the apes. Their heads were high and long. Their very powerful jaws jutted forward more than ours. They lacked a chin and had large bony ridges over the eyes. The forehead receded while, at the same time, the back of the head was well-developed. Their large head contained a similarly large brain that was, on average, 79 to 104 cubic inches (1300–1700 cm³). Thus the skull of the man found in France in La Ferrassie, not far from Eyzies in the Dordogne, had a capacity of 103 cubic inches (1681 cm³) versus an average of 85 cubic inches (1400 cm³) for modern humans. Neanderthal man had a big head.

Great Strength

Size? Probably average. The man from La Ferrassie, with a rather complete skeleton, could have been as tall as 5.6 feet (1.7 m). The woman discovered with him could have been no taller than 4.9 feet (1.48 m). The children (some have been discovered) seem to exhibit a slightly more rapid growth than do children today.

But if we judge them by their joints and their ligaments, Neanderthals were endowed with impressive strength. Their hands, with their thick joints, must have provided them with strength greater than ours. Hello, Mr. Neanderthal, but please do not shake hands too firmly . . .

Men, Real Men?

It is not surprising that this man was initially classified among the heavy-set brutes with ape-like features. Subsequently, humans that were older and with smaller skulls were discovered, thus bringing the Neanderthals closer to us. It appears that the paleontologists of the 1920s had unconsciously exaggerated the "great ape" characteristics of these poor humans. Today, everyone acknowledges that Neanderthals held themselves upright, from head to foot. Most scientists believe that Neanderthals are closely related to us, but it is not clear whether or not they are a distinct species from *Homo sapiens* or a subspecies: *Homo sapiens neanderthalensis*. In short, the Neanderthals have been rehabilitated. However, what were they like compared to modern humans, compared to us?

Men, women, and children held themselves upright the way we do and walked in the same way. Their big toes did not differ from the other toes of the foot, as far as we can tell.

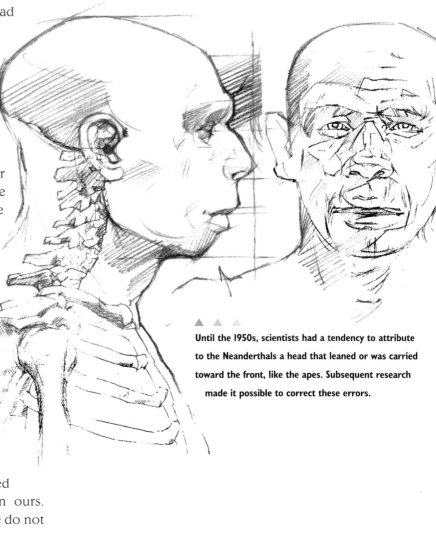

▲ ▲ ▲

Until the 1950s, scientists had a tendency to attribute to the Neanderthals a head that leaned or was carried toward the front, like the apes. Subsequent research made it possible to correct these errors.

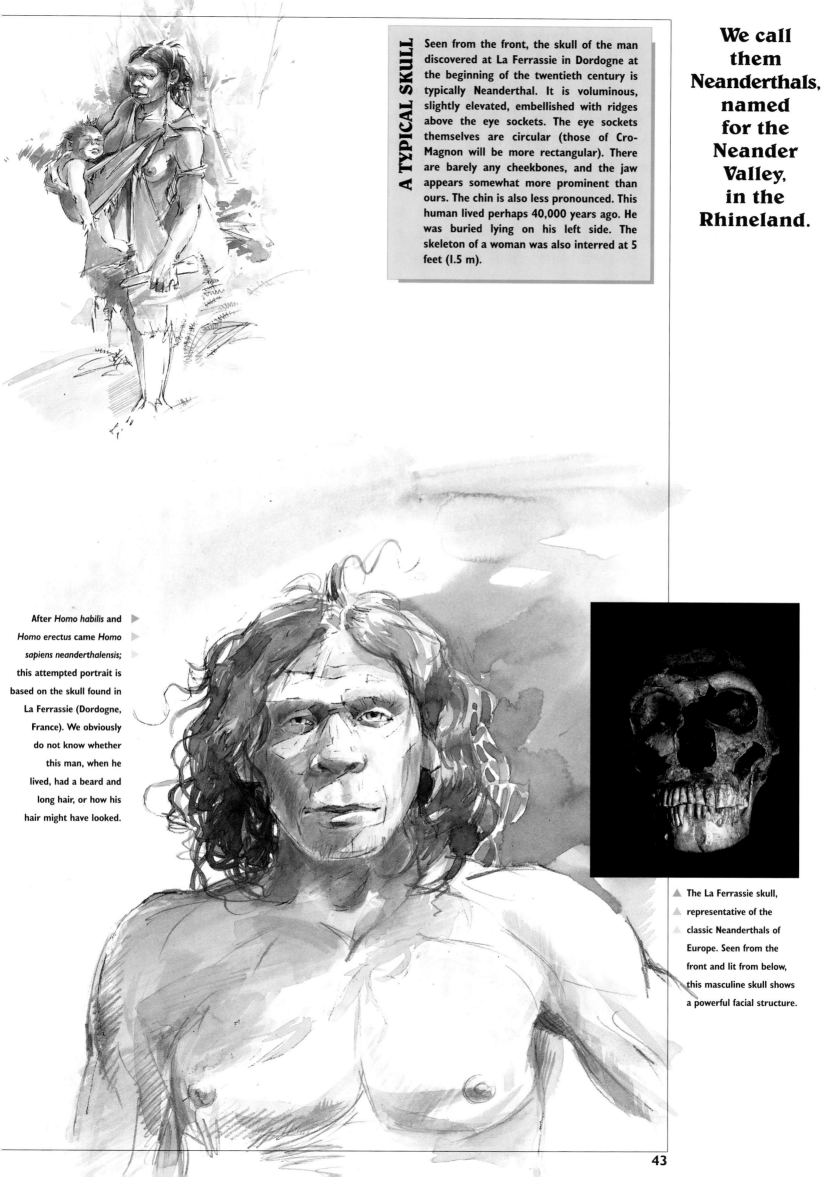

A TYPICAL SKULL

Seen from the front, the skull of the man discovered at La Ferrassie in Dordogne at the beginning of the twentieth century is typically Neanderthal. It is voluminous, slightly elevated, embellished with ridges above the eye sockets. The eye sockets themselves are circular (those of Cro-Magnon will be more rectangular). There are barely any cheekbones, and the jaw appears somewhat more prominent than ours. The chin is also less pronounced. This human lived perhaps 40,000 years ago. He was buried lying on his left side. The skeleton of a woman was also interred at 5 feet (I.5 m).

After *Homo habilis* and *Homo erectus* came *Homo sapiens neanderthalensis;* this attempted portrait is based on the skull found in La Ferrassie (Dordogne, France). We obviously do not know whether this man, when he lived, had a beard and long hair, or how his hair might have looked.

▲ The La Ferrassie skull, representative of the classic Neanderthals of Europe. Seen from the front and lit from below, this masculine skull shows a powerful facial structure.

THE EUROPEAN NEANDERTHAL

This human, with the features of and similarities (very great) and differences (marked) with modern man, is found only in Europe and the Near East.

The Neanderthals of Europe have unique characteristics. For example, the back of the skull projects into a "bun." It was believed at one time that these humans slowly migrated to the Near East. But paleontologists had to abandon this idea.

From the East to Europe?

The dates do not support this migration: Those Neanderthals of Europe are approximately as old as those of the Middle East. One interpretation is that there was a long period of evolution, a slow differentiation from *Homo erectus* all the way to the Neanderthals—in one place. The famous Mauer jawbone (400,000 to 600,000 years old) already has some Neanderthal characteristics. The famous Tautavel skull (found in the Arago cave, in the Corbieres), dates from approximately 400,000 years ago and shows a face that seems genuinely intermediary.

Atapuerca

The extraordinary Spanish site of Atapuerca provides us with another interpretation: The oldest remains (700,000 to 800,000 years old) show humans already distinct from *Homo erectus* while the most recent (300,000 years old) present the picture of a population that was almost Neanderthal. Thus, the occipital (the back of the head) from Swanscombe, in England, and especially that of Biache-Saint-Vaast (Pas-de-Calais, France) are quasi-Neanderthal. However, the Biache fossil is 180,000 years old, and no similar evolution is known in the Near East. This means that Neanderthals are not direct descendants of *Homo erectus*, and they probably are distinct from modern humans. Today, this remains an ongoing debate in paleoanthropology.

At the End of the World

These different "sapiens" would thus have slowly taken shape in the depth of the European periods. Why? Perhaps

A pure product of the European continent.

because of a certain European isolation, in this part of the world, for much of these hundreds of thousands of years. During the cold periods, in fact, an immense desert of ice covered the north of the continent. During their greatest extension, the ice of the north and that of the Alps would have only a very narrow corridor between them, which was probably not a very pleasant place to be. Elsewhere, ice covered the mountains of the Balkans, the Caucusus, and Armenia.

Son of Europe

No, communications must not have been very easy between the Near East and western Europe. This suggests that the children of *Homo erectus* evolved in isolation, which accounts for their progressive differentiation from the rest of the human population. The Neanderthals of the Near East would thus represent groups that left Europe during more clement periods, when the type was less pronounced. The migration would thus have moved from west to east, which means that Neanderthal is truly a pure product of the European continent. Later, modern humans would return the favor, in reverse, perhaps taking advantage of a slight "improvement" in climate.

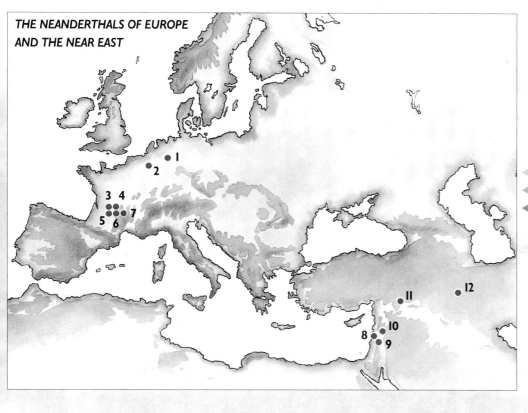

THE NEANDERTHALS OF EUROPE AND THE NEAR EAST

Some of the sites where Neanderthal fossils have been found:

1. Neanderthal
2. Spy
3. Le Moustier
4. Le Regourdou
5. Roc de Marsal
6. La Ferrassie
7. La Chapelle-aux-Saints
8. Tabun
9. Kebara
10. Amud
11. Dederiyeh
12. Shanidar

A European family 50,000 years ago, having just broken camp and departed for other locations, in search of other resources. It is certain that they did not just wander around. They followed a well-known route, regularly taken, perhaps every year. Sometimes, according to the climate, they changed the route: When a glaciation became established, they tended to double back toward the south, while during cold periods (and the permanently frozen ground) Europe north of the Loire and the Danube was effectively closed off.

1 Molodova
2 Le Moustier

THEY KNEW HOW
TO MAKE THINGS . . .

Fortunately for them, the Neanderthals knew how to use their large heads and their ten fingers.

The evidence of Neanderthals that remains proves real intellectual capacity and skills. The best example is their tools. The "Mousterian" technique—the name of the technique associated with Neanderthals—shows several ways of shaping stone. They obviously practiced the shaping of bifaces, inherited from earlier times, but the Mousterian bifaces are generally finer and more beautiful.

The "Levallois Technique"

They also knew an amazing technique. It consisted of fashioning the support case of the tool, the "core," in such a way that they did not have to strike it in order to obtain the tool itself. This supposes a good ability to plan and anticipate, and also a great deal of skill, as the blow of the hammer that detaches the tool from the nucleus (and thus creates it) required very great precision. That was not all: These Mousterians themselves developed a method that was long believed to be confined to modern man. It yielded standardized results, lengthened, with edges that could be used as they are or be used to make other tools. This "modern" technique was used alongside the others for more than 30,000 years, in the north of France and in Belgium.

Specialized Tools

Among specialized tools, the Mousterians had points, scrapers, and tools with serrated edges (denticulated) . . . . They pretty much had what they needed. Finally, they used other materials: wood—the imprint of a sharpened post was found while digging at a site in the Dordogne—and bone—there are shaped bones at some Mousterian sites. Some of these tools may have had handles. This is suggested by traces seen under the microscope on the portions of these tools opposite the active portion, that were not part of the shaped object.

First Pictures

Were modern humans alone in being able to "invent" pictures? As research has advanced and become more precise, investigators have discovered that there existed, long before the first intelligible representations, what may be called sketches, tests. These include, for example, traces of colors found at some sites, a carved and painted mammoth scapula, as in Molodova, in Ukraine. Other examples consist of small hollows, depressions on a stone, as at La Ferrassie in the Dordogne, or, in Charente, a bone engraved with groups of parallel and oblique lines from the cave at Petit Puymoyen. The images, we might say, were trying to emerge from the end of the big, muscular fingers of the Neanderthals. At the ends of their fingers and inside their heads were sketches and drawings of symbols.

A House Made of Mammoth

In the right bank of the Dnestr River, in

These imposing, strapping humans were not clumsy; quite the opposite.

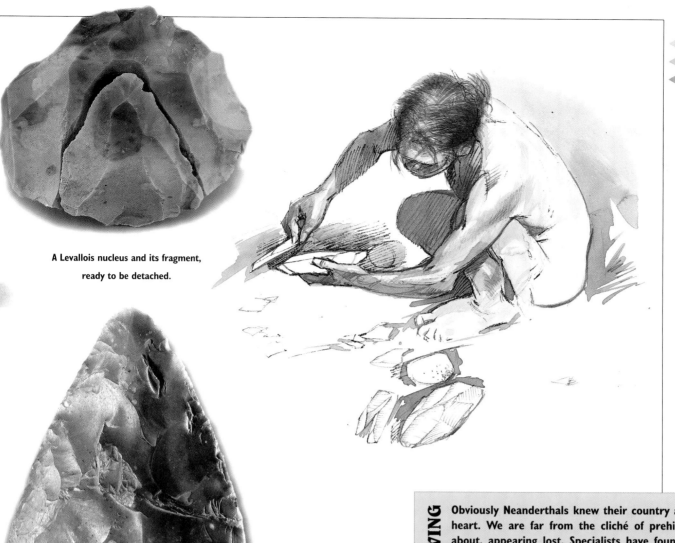

A Levallois nucleus and its fragment,
ready to be detached.

An excellent example of a triangular Mousterian biface.

Here are the three main ways of shaping stone at the time of the Neanderthals. From left to right: a typical biface shaping, by progressive shaping and removal of fragments; the Levallois shape, which "pre-forms" the piece on the core before detaching it; finally, the cutting of blades in series based on a well-prepared core.

MOVING Obviously Neanderthals knew their country and its resources by heart. We are far from the cliché of prehistoric man roaming about, appearing lost. Specialists have found evidence that the Neanderthals, the producers of Mousterian tools, knew perfectly where to find quality materials—good flint—and did not hesitate to undertake a long voyage to get some. Thus, approximately 100,000 years ago, at the height of the Mousterian era, the inhabitants of the Vaufrey shelter, near Sarlat in the Dordogne, France, used no fewer than six types of different rock to shape their tools. Although ordinary material was available on site, they would nevertheless go search for the best in a deposit located approximately 62 miles (100 km) to the north.

Ukraine, researchers discovered, at two different sites at the large deposit of Molodova, the remains of two huts that had been constructed of mammoth bones. One can almost call them houses. One of these structures consisted of 12 skulls, 15 tusks, 34 scapulas, and 351 epiphyses, or ends of long bones. It measured 17 by 27 feet (5 m by 8 m) and contained the remains of 15 fireplaces.

However advanced they appear to have been, we should not overidealize these brave Europeans of 50,000 years ago. The excavation of Mousterian sites has indicated that a certain disorder ruled their lives.

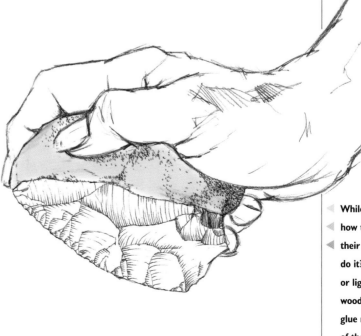

While Neanderthals knew how to put handles onto their tools, how did they do it? Did they use leather or ligaments to tie stone to wood and/or bone, or use glue made from the sap of the birch tree, which apparently was widely used much later on?

47

NEANDERTHAL ANIMALS

The Mousterian sites have yielded a large number of animal skeletons. The Neanderthals must have been efficient hunters, unafraid of large animals.

Aurochs

Reindeer

Cave bear

Mammoths and rhinoceros have been found among the Neanderthal trophies, in Molodova, Ukraine, for example. In a peat bog in Lehringen, Germany, an 8 foot (2.50 m) javelin made of yew wood was found . . . under the skeleton of a mammoth, estimated to be 120,000 years old.

Extinct Species

Some animals from prehistory were larger than their modern counterparts. In many cases, the species are extinct. Thus the so-called "cave" animals: cave bear (*Ursus spelaeus*), cave lion, cave hyena . . . . The aurochs was also an impressive animal, standing about 6 feet (1.80 m) tall at the shoulder. And the largest elephant in the ancient world before the last glaciation was the *Elephas trogontherii.* It could grow as large as 15 feet (4.5 m) in height.

The Influence of the Climate

The alternation of interglacial and glacial periods caused movements and changes in wildlife. Temperate wildlife was succeeded by so-called "cold" wildlife, with herds of reindeer reaching as far as the shores of the Mediterranean, and with them the partridge of the snows, polar foxes . . . brrr!

Cave cat

Ancient elephant

Hyena

Horse

Fossils found from South Africa as far as Israel show that another type of human had begun to separate itself from the older "erectus."

THE FIRST MODERN HUMANS

While the Neanderthals were finishing taking shape in Europe, a different type of humankind was emerging elsewhere. The skull structure was becoming lighter, the jaws less powerful, the chin more accentuated, the forehead more rounded, the ridges above the eye sockets flatter.

Modernity at 100,000 Years

In Zambia, Kabwe man, who for many years was considered an African Neanderthal, could actually have been either a late *Homo erectus* or a very primitive *Homo sapien* . . . more than 300,000 years ago. Kabwe man thus is evidence of changes in progress. Thus in South Africa, Border Cave man would prove to be between 90,000 and 110,000 years old. In Israel, Zuttiyeh man (Galilee), who shows similar characteristics, also dates back more than 200,000 years. Finally, the cave of Qafzeh (also in Israel) sheltered humans who were almost "modern," that is, very close to us, at a date of 95,000 years. One of them was 6 feet, 2 inches (1.88 m) tall.

A Certain Technical Intelligence

A remarkable fact: These humans fashioned their tools in the Mousterian style, just like the first Neanderthal. They probably led the same kind of life, had the same thoughts, in any event evidenced the same technical intelligence. Those from the Border Cave used the Levallois method. What we have here is proof that types of tools and types of humans should not be too closely connected. Many thousands of years would pass before these moderns would change in innovative ways.

Where Did They Come From?

When did this change take place? How did we become modern? We do not know. The exact area where the moderns could have appeared remains unknown. All of these quasi-moderns from 90,000 to 130,000 were dispersed over a wide area—exactly like the first humans. This contradicts the affirmations of some biologists, who contend that a single individual could have carried the mutation or mutations from which all of humanity would arise.

A Controversial Origin

Biologists have become involved. Just as specialists in chromosomes have reconstructed a primate genealogy, some biologists have created their own genealogy in which humans are descended from a single, female individual, an "African Eve," who would thus be at the origin of humanity. This may certainly be a way of finding the biblical Eve, but it is not accepted with enthusiasm by most scientists. They do not see why the populations of Africa and the Near East could not have diverged from the *Homo erectus* forms to the modern forms, as the Neanderthals did in Europe; however, there was no Neanderthal Eve—we do not know where she should be situated in time. In Africa and in the Near East, there were perhaps thousands of Eves and Adams.

▲ At the entrance of the cave ▲ of Qafzeh, which opens in ▲ the side of Mount Qafzeh, or Precipice Mountain, near the village of Nazareth. Remains of modern humans, 95,000 years old, were discovered there.

Thousands of Eves at the origin of modern man.

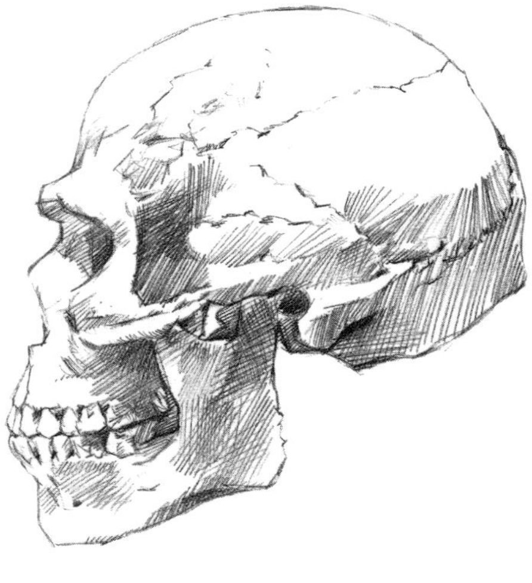

Portrait of Skhul man, based on his reconstructed skull.

AN AFRICAN EVE?

Biologists have studied the DNA from modern men and women from all over the world. They were able to establish relationships and, more and more precisely, to establish a genealogical tree based on the more or less major differences among current populations. This led them to Africa, where their molecular clock suggests an "African Eve" lived perhaps 200,000 years ago. Criticism is not lacking, however. On the one hand, mitochondrial DNA is mainly transmitted by women. We are thus obliged to end up with an Eve. This is no joke! On the other hand, the genealogy based solely on DNA does not reflect exactly the real evolution of organisms. Many other factors have played a part and, for the moment at least, discoveries on site have not confirmed this precise origin in any respect.

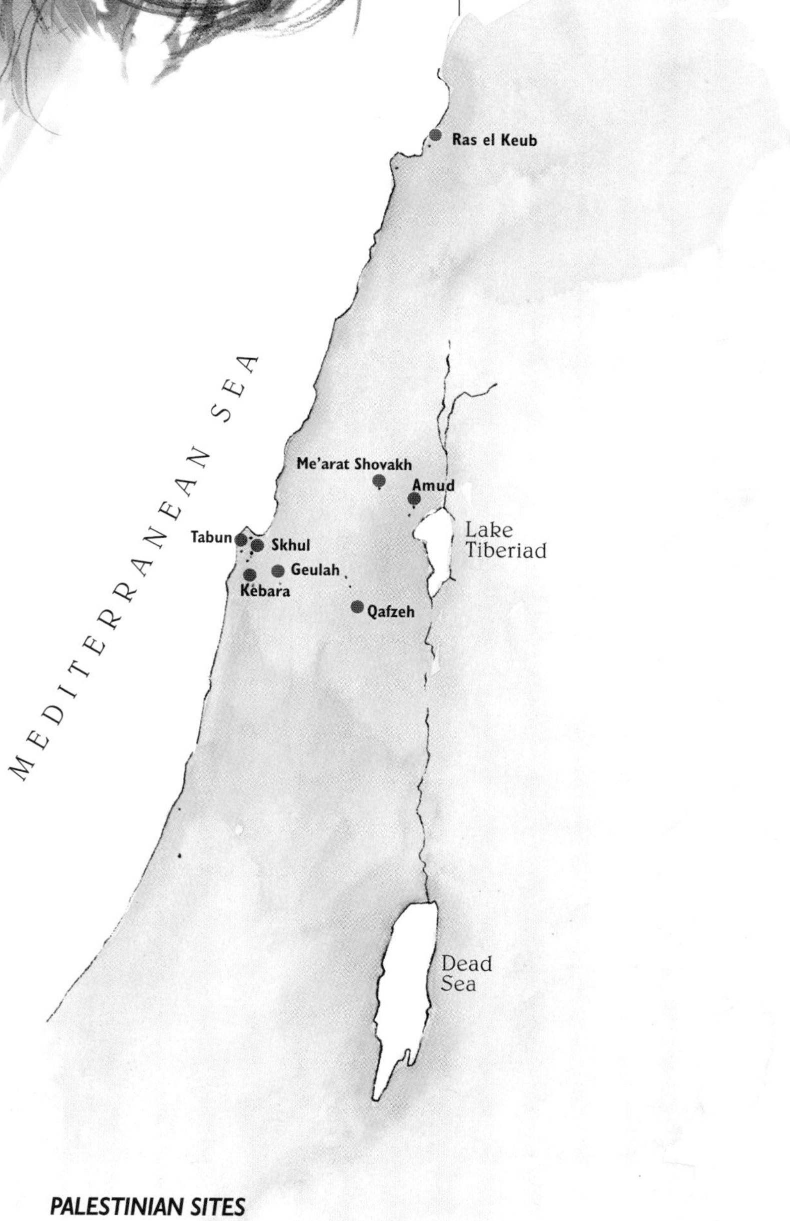

MEDITERRANEAN SEA

Ras el Keub

Me'arat Shovakh
Amud
Tabun
Skhul
Geulah
Kebara
Qafzeh

Lake Tiberiad

Dead Sea

PALESTINIAN SITES

1 Cro-Magnon
2 Predmost
3 Sungir

WHERE THEY BEGAN TO BURY THE DEAD

The oldest known tomb–it can be dated at 95,000 years of age–was discovered near Nazareth, in Israel. At least three people were buried there, at the entrance to the cave of Qafzeh.

A woman was placed on her left side, curled up. At her feet, in the same pit, were crammed the bones of a child of six. An adolescent thirteen years old was buried on his back, the hands brought around from each side of the neck. A deer antler was placed there, across his neck, just below the hands.

The First Tombs

A somewhat older tomb that dates back approximately 100,000 years was found 22 miles (35 km) from there, in the cave of Skhul, near Mount Carmel. Yet another was nearby—that of Kebara, approximately 60,000 years old. This is also the age that was given to the tombs at Shanidar, in Iraq, where a nine-year-old child may have been buried with flowers (traces of pollen were found).

Who were these people who were buried? In Qafzeh and in Skhul, they were anatomically modern humans, *Homo sapiens sapiens*. In Shanidar and Kebara, they were Neanderthals. Our current state of knowledge suggests that it would thus have been the modern humans of Qafzeh who first buried their dead, and also to have explored the beliefs and the thought processes connected with this practice. The Neanderthals would have followed shortly thereafter.

And in Europe?

It is said that an entire Neanderthal family was buried at La Ferrassie (Dordogne): a man, a woman, two children (of ten and three years), newborns, even a fetus. Above the pit where the three-year-old child had been placed, there was a stone slab on which holes had been hollowed out. Who, then, had wanted these rituals 40,000 years ago? To what fears, what certainties, did they respond?

How do you determine whether a human burial was intentional or not? Couldn't these apparently deliberate burials just as easily have been people left where they died, with no ceremony? Perhaps many remains presented as "buried" were not. But three elements make it possible to consider the tomb probable or certain. First, the skeleton was found almost complete, with the bones still connected. This means that they were protected, both from animals and from bad weather that could have dispersed the bones. Then, it appears that the pit remained visible: The refilling stands out clearly on the surrounding ground. Finally, objects were deposited in the tomb alongside the dead person. Thus we can reduce our chances of erring in saying that the humans of Qafzeh (Israel) and those of La Ferrassie (France) were freely and ceremoniously buried between 40,000 and 90,000 years ago.

A deer
antler
across the
neck.

THE FIRST GRAVES IN THE NEAR EAST AND IN EUROPE

In the entryway were interred a young woman in a flexed position and a child, laid on top of her feet. This double grave, estimated at 95,000 years old, is one of the most ancient discovered to date.

1   Le Regourdou
2   La Ferrassie
3   La Chapelle-aux-Saints
4   Skhul
5   Qafzeh
6   Kebara
7   Shanidar

CRO-MAGNON
AND OTHERS

"Homo sapiens sapiens": Larger, with less massive structures than their predecessors, they emerged from the depths of Africa, more than 100,000 years ago. They were also found in Palestine. And elsewhere?

I n 1868, a railroad line was under construction in the southwest of France, in the Dordogne, near a small village that then was unknown: Les Eyzies. The track had been built alongside a cliff (which is always the case), and earth and stone were needed to build it.

Chance and Discovery

The earth and stones were taken from all around and specifically from a recess at the foot of the cliff. This, it turned out, was the Cro-Magnon shelter. Bones appeared—the remains of four adults at least, of a newborn, and of others. One of these skeletons became the famous "Cro-Magnon man." Dead at approximately fifty years of age, having lost all of his teeth and crippled with rheumatism, he officially represents the "modern" population of a large portion of Europe and North Africa some 35,000 years ago.

Even Taller Men

These Cro-Magnons were found from Russia (in Sungir) and the Czech Republic (in Predmost) as far as Morocco (in Mechta el Arbi). They were tall. The average height of known males reached 5 feet 10 inches (1.74 m), and many were taller than 6 feet 1 inch (1.85 m). They had high foreheads, somewhat rectangular eye sockets, prominent cheeks, and pronounced chins. They still retained some distant reminders of *Homo erectus*

in the cranium, which we have lost. Although less stocky than Neanderthals, they were powerfully muscled.

The skull of Cro-Magnon man; already us, with many similarities.

Flint Blades and Bone Assegais

They had advanced technically. It is with them or with their Palestinian ancestors that the first tools known as Aurignacian made their appearance. (Aurignac is a site in the southwest of France, near the Pyrenees.) These tools are based on the production in series of strips from blocks of flint (cores) carefully prepared. This "blade" work was accompanied by another advance: fine points made of bone that must have served to arm the assegais, a hardwood spear. Finally, the arrival of these

ILLNESSES, ALREADY

Bones can often tell us a great deal about the activities of prehistoric man. They can even, on occasion, reveal some of their illnesses: those that affected bone. The La Ferrassie (Dordogne) skeleton shows deformations on the feet related to a squatting position. There are also traces of degenerative diseases (spondyloses), from which Cro-Magnon man, for example, suffered. His deformed bones may then show that he would have spent much of his time sitting down. This type of illness, found in many bones, suggests that prehistoric humans led a rather sedentary life if, at the same time, their bones also show few signs of trauma—few serious cases but lots of small accidents, such as dislocations, sprains, fractures of the forearm . . . . However, post-accidental ossifications, or changes in the bone mass, show that the patient often successfully recovered. A life sitting down, but not without activity.

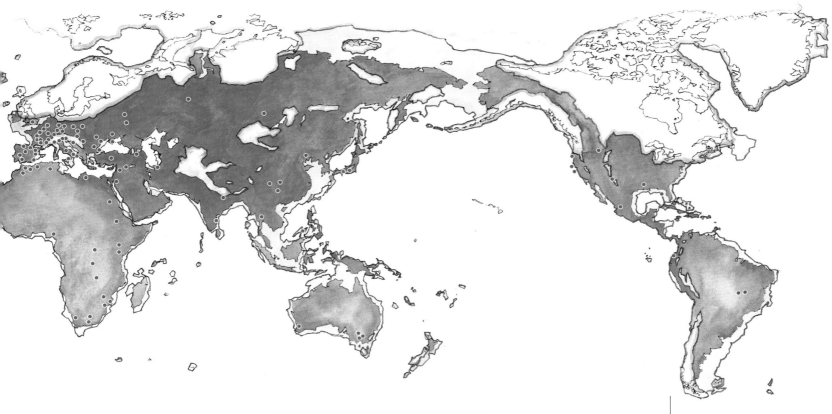

Aurignacians was accompanied by a veritable explosion of images, of figures that were painted and, occasionally, engraved, or sculpted—not at all like the earlier sketches.

The Question of Asia

These modern humans also reached Asia. How were they "modernized" in Indonesia and in China? Anthropologists have raised these questions based on the few available remains. In Java, Ngandong man has a rather elevated skull and smaller ridges above the eye sockets. Remains found in Sambungmachan present a more archaic appearance. The same is true in China, where the Dali fossil is rather more like an "evolved *Homo erectus*," while that of Maba is more modern. The question was thus asked whether in Asia, as in Africa, there had been a progressive passage from the ancient to the modern type with no migration necessary, Asia having completed its evolution in an autonomous manner. The question has remained open for a long time.

Whatever one's opinion of the predecessors of Cro-Magnon, it must be admitted that the latter pushed skill and invention further. This is shown by this Cro-Magnon woman, sewing in her tent 15,000 to 20,000 years ago.

These are the people of 40,000 to 100,000 years ago from whom modern humans are descended.

Another Coexistence

In fact, to answer the question it would be necessary to date these fossils, specifically in connection with those from Africa and the Near East. Not an easy task, given the state of the sites where they were found and the age of these finds. A part of a response came from new dating conducted in Java: Ngandong man is similar to *Homo erectus*, or maybe advanced *Homo erectus*.

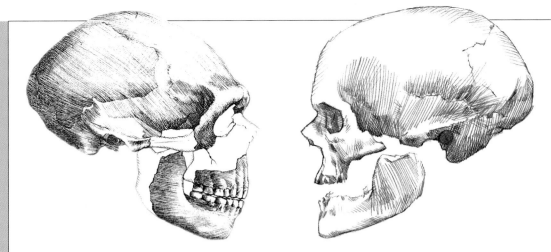

*Something tragic had occurred:
A population had disappeared.
The Neanderthals had populated
Europe for such a long time. Now
they were extinct. Why?*

EIGHT THOUSAND YEARS OF COEXISTENCE

Cro-Magnon people arrived, with all their technical skills. A real Aurignacian, with spear points and everything else, existed 45,000 years ago in Bulgaria. Five thousand years later, our Cro-Magnon Aurignacians found themselves in the north of Spain, in Catalonia, and in the Cantabrian region. In five thousand years, these people had crossed the Neanderthal-Mousterian continent almost from one end to the other. Average rate: one-fourth mile (600 m) per year. Prehistorically speaking, this was lightning speed.

Was There a Massacre?
What took place during this encounter? The first explanation, obviously, was that of a massacre: Cro-Magnon could have easily eliminated Neanderthal, who were poorly equipped and less cunning. But it seems that 10,000 years after the arrival of Cro-Magnon, Neanderthal was still there. The dates prove it. Zero points for the massacre solution.

Living Side by Side
In much of Europe, Mousterian, thus Neanderthal, sites were contemporary with Aurignacian, thus Cro-Magnon, sites. The facts are there. During the long millennia, the two populations coexisted. This observation tells us a great deal. The coexistence of the two was possible. But how did it express itself? What could have been the relationship between these two peoples?

In Which Neanderthal Adapts
Another culture had existed, exactly at the same time. Known as the industry of Châtelperron (French site in the Allier), it involved the production of blades, the fashioning of very fine points; but it also appears to have been very similar to the old Mousterian. For a long time, it was not known that this population made these blades. Then came the discovery of Saint-Césaire in 1979, in the Charentes (France): a skull in small pieces and a skeleton in the middle of a layer of Châtelperron tools. It revealed itself to be . . . Neanderthal.

Had Acculturation Taken Place?
Faced with these new arrivals who were better equipped, the natives might have progressed by adopting some of the new techniques. The evidence from Châtelperron suggests that there were contacts, even if we do not know their exact nature. Châtelperron industry could in this way have resulted in a kind of acculturation of the Neanderthals, without eliminating the possibility that these humans themselves might have been capable of innovation. It had its own territory, from Burgundy and Allier as far as the Basque region of Spain, and it appears to have flourished there. Two French sites are known, in the Dordogne and in Carats, where layers of Châtelperron cover layers of Aurignacian, where the Neanderthal succeeded the Cro-Magnon, which could almost make one think of expansion. An acculturation of the same type could have taken place in Central Europe with the tools of Szeletien, discovered in Hungary.

▲ A Châtelperron point: final evidence of the Neanderthals or first modern tool?

What took place between these two peoples?

Extinction all the Same

Elsewhere, the Mousterian continued, but declined. Perhaps the two peoples had begun to coexist; however, there are far fewer Mousterian sites than before. Even the culture of Châtelperron, after an initial growth, weakened. It ended by disappearing and the Aurignacian took over. Some late Mousterian sites still existed around 30,000 years ago in the Rhone Valley and further, at the end, in Andalusia: In the Zaffaraya cave (at an altitude of 3,630 feet, or 1100 m), hunters of ibex passed several times. They used the Mousterian tools. They lit a fire. In the entryway, an indisputably Neanderthal jawbone, belonging to someone young, dated at approximately 33,000 years, while the last Mousterian layer is situated between 26,000 and 29,000 years. This end of Europe was apparently the site of the end of a lengthy history.

CHATELPERRONIAN SITES FROM CENTRAL FRANCE TO NORTHERN SPAIN

Arcy-sur-Cure

Châtelperron

Quinçay

Saint-Césaire

La Chaise

la Quina

Fontéchevade

La Ferrassie

Labgerie-Haute

Cro-Magnon

Le Piage

Roc-de-Combe

Cueva Morin

Saint-Pierre-d'Irube

Isturitz

Gatzarria

Montmaurin

Aurignac

Le Portel

Agut

THE CONCEPT OF TERRITORY

The peoples known as hunters do not have the same concept of territory as do agricultural peoples. They do not feel that they own the area in which they complete their annual circuit. They have bigger ideas. This view makes it understandable that the great Aurignacians could have rather quickly crossed a European continent, whose population was widely dispersed, without any of those already there thinking of preventing them from doing so. However, the Mousterians seem to have had territories. There was another, known as the "Acheulian tradition" that was unknown in the Mediterranean regions. This was a culture such as the Châtelperronian that existed only in the area from Burgundy to the Basque region. Later on, the other strange culture known as Solutrean would only exist from the north of Spain to the center of France. The available evidence suggests that territories, areas, could have been defined, at least as far as techniques are concerned.

THE POPULATING OF AUSTRALIA

Continent of surprises, Australia offers the extraordinary example of an almost current prehistory and one that goes much further back in time than was once thought.

At the time when the seas were low, Australia and New Guinea formed a single, vast continent called Sahul. However, even then, a sea separated it from Asia.

Immense Territories

To populate this vast continent, some group of people had to make a successful maritime crossing. And it was believed, of course, that the crossing could only have been accomplished much later, when men were able to venture out onto the sea. Australian prehistory must therefore be very recent—a few thousand years old at most. Two discoveries overturned these ideas.

Mungo Lake

On the shores of a now-dry quaternary lake, Mungo Lake (not far from the Darling River in New South Wales), a large fossil dune eroded by winds revealed superimposed archeological strata (a stratigraphy) of stone tools, charcoal, and bones . . . among which were human bones. Research begun at the end of the 1960s led to the discovery, among others, of the remains of two people, a young woman of rather frail appearance (we

have one-quarter of her bones) and a man who suffered from arthritis and had bad teeth . . . . Both are indubitably modern. The site and the bones were dated. The sites were occupied about 32,000 years ago, with the man's skeleton somewhere between 28,000 and 32,000 years old, and the young woman's between 24,500 and 26,500 years.

Willandra Lakes

Many questions can be asked about the human fossils of the Willandra lakes: a deposit of the remains of 135 humans, some of whom had slender builds (like those of Mungo Lake) and others who were much more robust. All date back at least 15,000 years and some up to 35,000 years. Who were these first Australians, and were there not perhaps some descendants of the old *Homo erectus* among them? One example, labeled Hominid number 50 from Willandra lakes, has been found to be at least 35,000 and perhaps more than 40,000 years old. This specimen has a skull with a rather flat front whose walls are 15 to 19 millimeters thick.

The Realm of the Image

But Australian prehistory is, above all, a

The oldest known maritime crossing.

In the Australian bush, in the heart of the Uluru National Park.

THE OLDEST PREHISTORIC
SITES IN AUSTRALIA

PHILIPPINES

PACIFIC OCEAN

MALAYSIA

BORNEO

NEW GUINEA

SUMATRA

CELEBES

JAVA

INDIAN OCEAN

Current
coastal limits

Arnhem
Land
Malakunanya II

Northern
Territory

AUSTRALIA

Willandra Lakes
Mungo Lake

New South Wales

Coastal limits
20,000 years ago

Migration Routes

TASMANIA

celebration, thanks to its paintings. Here, again, it was possible to date the paintings in relation to archeological strata near or covered by them. Investigators showed that some figures from sites in the north could be approximately 30,000 years old. At a site called Malakunanya II, in the Arnhem Land, a red block—hematite—was found in sands that can be traced to about 50,000 years ago. These dates when considered with those of Mungo, show an Australia that was inhabited for much longer than had been believed. This shift made it necessary to imagine people crossing the Timor Strait 40,000 or 50,000 years ago or more. This broke the old record for inventing navigation . . . . But perhaps it is necessary to go back even further.

The Dream Time

In Jinmium, a site in the northwest, marked rocks were found that could be between 58,000 and 75,000 years old. Hollows dug in a large rock date back between 75,000 to 116,000 years. And the oldest stratum is around 176,000 years old . . . . But here, the dates must be confirmed because not all investigators agree about the method used. Nevertheless, the find is

still an indication of great age. 60,000 years? Perhaps 100,000 years? If these dates are correct, we must ask what kind of human was he, the first to reach this continent? This period for which the Australian aborigines have the lovely name, "the dream time," has perhaps not finished astonishing us . . . and making us dream.

Dated at 40,000 years of age, the figures of the Panaramittee (southern Australia) type are perhaps the oldest representations in the world. On these engravings carved on a stone slab in the ground are kangaroo tracks.

1 Chauvet Cave
2 Cosquer Cave
3 Gargas Cave
4 Hehlenstein Stadel

THE EXPLOSION **OF THE IMAGE**

30,000 years ago, on three continents, the image was born. We would like to know what was taking place in the minds of humans, from what new perspective they viewed the world.

First there were the Australians who carved out hollows and used color—we do not know why—60,000-plus years ago. These were the people who crushed some red 50,000 years ago, who carved who knows what on the bones and the stones, in many places, well before they created their first images.

Distant Roots

In Australia, the carved oval of Wharton Hill dates back more than 40,000 years; in Panaramittee North, a curved line is 43,000 years old and a series of complicated carvings approximately 47,000 years old. In Europe, the Neanderthals carved holes in the stone slab of a tomb, carving lines on bones—some carefully parallel, others fanning out—whether in Crimea, in Germany, in France, or in the Czech Republic. And we also find, at their sites, traces of color here and there. In many places throughout the world a slow preparation reveals itself. Tests? Trials?

The First Images

But here the image is born—powerful, perfect, on two continents and perhaps on three. That is at least how it looks to us. After thousands of years of trial and error, suddenly, masterpieces appeared. We will, perhaps, never know if these people painted their bodies, their faces, or if they had painted on skins or peels, or if they had sculpted wood for several thousand years . . .

In Europe

The discovery of the Chauvet cave in southeast France, then the dating of its paintings, had an explosive impact. Here, in these images, all awkwardness disappears, is unknown, from animals drawn from life, painted 30,000 to 32,000 years ago. Drawing has not improved since then. Ten thousand years later came the creation of the splendid animals of the Cosquer cave, located near Marseille, and today inundated, in part, by the rising of the sea. In southern Germany, the animal and human

Already famous, the horses of Cosquer cave, near Marseille, have been dated at 19,000 years.

statuettes in bone from the caves of Vogelherd and Geissenklosteris, which stand out as remarkable achievements, are also around 30,000 years old.

In Australia

On the other side of the world, early Australians were not resting. In the sites in the north, there are ten layers of works superimposed on the walls of shelters. The oldest may be 30,000 years old. They depict animals and mythological beings, drawn in red, in the style both precise and rather wild that characterizes this continent.

At the Gates of Asia and of Africa

There is, perhaps, a sanctuary 30,000 years old in the Negev Desert: forty arranged blocks of flint, some of which resemble human shapes, and designs of pebbles on the ground, as well as Aurignacian tools. To be confirmed . . .

Finally, in Africa, where research is less advanced, the discoveries are multiplying (more than 300 sites in Botswana). In a site in Namibia named Apollo XI, a fragment of rock bears the drawing of a herbivore. The archeological stratum has been dated at 27,000 years.

On All Continents

The image was thus born almost everywhere. More or less completed, realistic or symbolic, it appeared in fine form on three continents several millennia apart—almost at the same time in prehistoric terms. Why? No one knows. What new way of looking does this suggest and permit of the world? What kinds of explanations and certitudes does the image suggest? In any event it seems closely linked to the strange condition of *Homo sapiens sapiens*. But note: with each decade have come new discoveries that profoundly affect our notion of the birth of the image. Any explanation can therefore only be provisional, because it will likely change.

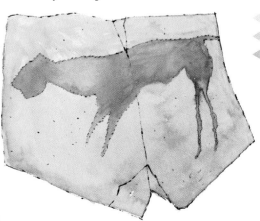

One of the oldest known images: "the herbivore" from the Namibian site Apollo XI. It may be 27,000 years old.

Among the masterpieces of the first images in Europe: a human being with the head of an animal, found in the Hohlenstein Stadel cave, in Germany, made more than 30,000 years ago.

There are approximately two hundred images of hands in the Gargas (France) cave that can be dated at 26,000 years.

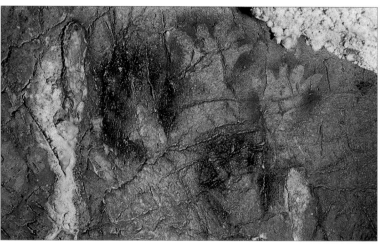

A very long preparation and then, suddenly . . .

CHAUVET CAVE: THE DISCOVERY

It was beautiful and cold in the gorges of the Ardeche on Sunday, December 18, 1994, around 3:00 P.M. Experienced speleologists, among them Jean-Marie Chauvet, had decided to have another look at a frequently traveled area, particularly a small opening 32 by 12 inches (80 by 30 cm). After quite a bit of gymnastics, they encountered a large room, but also a sheer drop of 33 feet (10 m). U-turn! Night had fallen, it was not warm . . . but the idea that someone else could have came that way made them decide to return. They unrolled the rope ladder, then advanced to the large room, following in each other's footsteps in order to leave only one track. A second room, still bigger, had bear skeletons on the floor and dozens of basins remaining from wintering. Further on, in a narrower gallery, in the light of the explorer's headlamps, there suddenly emerged two lines of red ocher on the wall. When the explorers turned around, a small red mammoth leapt into view. Amazing visions followed one after another: a red bear, a black rhinoceros . . .

The lamps began to grow weak, our speleologists left, but, although tired, they departed dazzled. What they had just discovered is in the same category as the most famous groups of images. The following Sunday, they made more discoveries with other speleologists. They ate nothing while inside in order not to risk contaminating the site, but they did uncork a bottle of champagne, brought expressly for the occasion . . .

1 **Pedra Furada**
2 **Monte Verde**
3 **Meadowcroft**
4 **Pendejo**

THE ENIGMA
OF THE AMERICAS

When did humans really discover America? Noting the disagreements of prehistorians on this subject, it must be said that this first discovery could not have been easy.

I n the sixteenth century, when the Spanish conquistadors arrived in the "West Indies," that is, in Mexico and Peru, they found (and destroyed) ancient and flourishing civilizations. But how old were these civilizations? When, in the nineteenth century, the British and French colonists settled in North America, they met, displaced, and also destroyed native peoples, both farmers and hunters, who had been there since when? In the twentieth century, ethnologists in Patagonia and in Tierra del Fuego encountered Indians (now extinct) who lived by fishing and gathering—as they always had. But when did this "always" begin?

11,000 Years or More?

It is forever, in any event, since the beginnings of research on this continent, that the prehistorians have disagreed on the date of the "first" Americans. Two opposing schools exist on this matter of "forever": the "11,000 years" and the "more than that." The 11,000 years is the age of the "Paleo-Indians" of North America, with many sites, subtle techniques for making tools in obsidian, and very beautiful striated points. [Before this culture, called Clovis (named for a site in New Mexico, see p. 80–81) the supporters of a recent American prehistory will acknowledge practically nothing.]

Numerous Claims

There are numerous claims for a much older prehistory: 24,000 years in Mexico, 50,000 or even 80,000 years in the southwest United States, more than 40,000 years in Brazil . . . . But all, or almost all, have been questioned. Beyond the fateful 11,000 years, a kind of unhappy fate seems to have plagued the American sites. The stratigraphies are complex, when they exist, and the remains difficult to identify or to date.

45,000 Years in Brazil?

In the Pendejo cave (as well as in New Mexico) investigators believe that they have found worked stones and bones, along with hair and fingerprints that may be more than 30,000 years old.

The majority of visitors do not believe this is correct. In South America, the Brazilian site Pedra Furada has not only provided rupestrian painting and archeological strata dated at approximately 11,000 years, but it has also yielded what appear to be worked stones and charcoal, which were estimated to be 30,000 and 40,000 years old. But were the stones in question really worked? Didn't the charcoal come from natural fires?

Monte Verde

Nevertheless, among the sites considered to be "sure" is one in Monte Verde, Chile: a group of dwellings was found on a peat bog. The dates assigned are around 13,000 years. Two thousand years before the people of Clovis, humans already lived 6,200 miles (10,000 km) further

By what route did the first "Americans" arrive? They must have traveled across the Bering Strait. This was easy during the period of glaciation because the decrease in the sea level created an enormous continental area, over 621 miles (1,000 km) wide. But then the travelers would have confronted immense ice fields. Perhaps there existed, as it is now thought, a corridor free of ice between the ice sheet of the Rocky Mountains and the Laurentians? They could have passed through during three periods: from 12,000 to 15,000 years, from 25,000 to 30,000 years, and from 60,000 to 75,000 years. The middle period seems the most reasonable. But another solution would be that they came by boat and descended along the coast using coastal navigation.

Is there a paradise behind the ice?

Is there a passageway?

south! How much time did they need to reach this region from the north? And from the Bering Strait, which appears to have been the means of entry into America from Asia? Moreover, fireplaces, concentrations of coal, and stone that has perhaps been worked have been dated at 33,000 years—almost a scandal for the supporters of 11,000 years.

The New World Is Not So New!

With the Monte Verde findings, prehistorians quickly began their research in the north. In the United States, the Meadowcroft shelter in Pennsylvania was inhabited at least 12,800 years ago. In the west of the country, dating by radiocarbon was begun on microscopic organisms (algae, for example) trapped by the layers of patina that covered the worked stones and rock engravings (petroglyphs) in desert areas. Radiocarbon tests yield an age of 16,000 and 18,000 years for the petroglyphs of the Petrified Forest in Arizona, and 26,000 years for the worked pieces from the Mohave Desert. These results were severely criticized and are still not confirmed . . . . But finally, the New World could have been a bit less new than was previously believed. Criticism not withstanding, the number of sites that have given dates of 20,000 years and more in the United States, in Mexico (Tiapacoya), in Brazil (Pedra Furada), or in Peru is becoming significant.

A real New World, preserved by humans for two million years.

THE VESTIGES OF MONTE VERDE

Monte Verde is a particularly rich site. It was covered by a peat bog: The peat preserved the organic matter. Estimated to be 13,000 years old, the twelve dwellings for which remains have been found had bases of branches supported by vertical posts.

Under the peat, wood was preserved: posts of houses, mortars near hallways . . . . On the branches of the roof, the trace of animal skin still remained. Worked sticks, like gouges, were also collected, along with a scraper that still had its handle, as well as leaves, grains, shriveled fruit, and tubers. Under these remains, others were found that seem even older.

EUROPE AND NORTH AMERICA
DURING THE ICE AGE

Are you familiar with the tundra? Today it is found in the north of Russia, in Siberia, in the north of Canada, in Alaska.

The tundra consists of vast stretches without trees, except for some willows and dwarf birches. In winter, there is snow and frost. In the summer, the ground remains frozen down deep (the phenomenon of permafrost) and unfrozen on the surface. This makes it difficult for the water to run off, which causes the formation of enormous marshes.

This Was Not the Great North

But please note, in prehistoric times, all of Europe was not tundra, only the territories located near the ice. Modern tundras extend around the polar circle. However, at the height of glacial periods, the European ice sheet reached as far as London, Bremen, Berlin . . . and the North American ice sheet, that of the "Laurentians," reached the site where New York stands today and covered that of Chicago. Finally, the length of the days, the relationship between the seasons and the amount of sunlight, was not the same as it is in the Great North today.

A Completely Different Environment

July in the basin of Paris was doubtless cooler than today, but it was certainly warmer than it is in the modern tundras of Canada or Siberia. Humans of this period thus lived in an environment for which there is no contemporary equivalent. Only the region of Newfoundland and Labrador, located at lower latitudes and bordered by cold ocean currents, can recall, to a certain extent, what the Paris basin and the plains of the Midwest must have been like 20,000 years ago.

Frozen Ground of Belgium

Near glaciers, in what were called the periglacial zones, life certainly must not have been very pleasant. Traces of permafrost have been found in the north of France, throughout Belgium, in central Germany, and in the Great Plains of the United States. The same regions also contain large deposits of loess, or sand that is separated from barren ground and transported by the wind. They date back to the glacial times. Prehistoric sites are, moreover, uncommon in these areas for this period of time.

The Steppe but also the Trees

But it is sufficient to move a bit south to find conditions more favorable for plant and animal life, and thus for the support of humans. In the Paris basin and the south of Germany, the steppes dominated, but they were not completely barren. Almost all sites have yielded pollen from trees: birches and pines particularly, as well as willows. These trees must have lodged themselves in small valleys, against sheltered and sunny slopes. Willows and alders could be found along the rivers. Still further south, the proportion of trees increased. This did not prevent herds of deer from living as far as the foot of the Pyrenees, or saiga antelopes (today in the steppes of Central Asia) from crossing the Aquitaine. There were also some stags, some boars . . . . Musk ox did not reach beyond the Ardennes.

Sometimes, however, it was mild.

Today the Rhine is at the heart of European industrial activity. But on these same riverbanks, similar feasts must have taken place 20,000 years ago.

THE STRANGE GEOGRAPHY OF EUROPE DURING THE LAST GLACIATION

OCEAN

BLACK SEA

MEDITERRANEAN SEA

Varied Fauna

Above all, in Europe as well as in North America, this was the time of the great herds: deer or caribou, bison (from Europe or America), horses, to which were added small troops of aurochs and mammoths. Put all of these together, mix them toward the south with a bit of temperate fauna (like the trees, there always were some) and, say the zoologists, you have the richest, most diverse, and even contrasting fauna that ever lived in these regions.

THE GREAT BOOK OF SOIL

The climates of prehistory can be read in the soil. Looking only at the Ice Age, the sediments and rocks retain many traces of the poor treatment to which they were subjected by frosts and thaws: massive mud slides the length of the thawed slopes, broken rock, movements of sediment in the areas where the ground remained frozen below and thawed in the summer only on the surface . . . . These are, in effect, signatures of a truly cold climate and a certain proximity of glaciers, encountered in a large portion of northwest Europe.

The ground can also contain fossil pollens. Each one different, these pollens make it possible to learn about the vegetation of a particular period: the ratio of grasses to trees, pines to oaks, dandelions . . . . The pattern of pollens can also recount the history of the vegetation in the sediments, where it is well distributed in superimposed layers in the peat bogs and the archeological sites at numerous strata. Pollens were useful, for example, in determining the number of climatic fluctuations that took place during the approximately 100,000 years of the last glaciation.

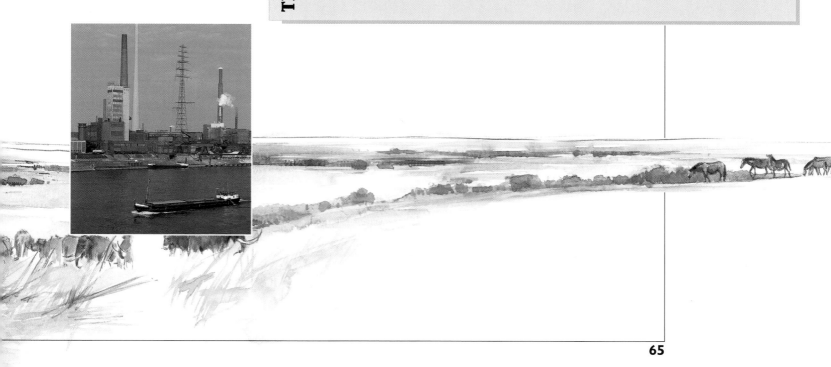

THE PREHISTORY OF ELEPHANTS

The mammoth, that prehistoric elephant covered with lots of hair, with its hump on the head and its doubly curved tusks, has excited the imagination since the time it was first discovered, in the 17th and 18th centuries.

Prehistoric humans probably dreamed about them, drawing them on the walls of caves, in Rouffignac (Dordogne), in Arcy-sur-Cure (Burgundy), and in many other places . . . . But what they drew was real.

The mammoth descended from even older types of elephants. It differs from its predecessors in its extraordinary adaptation to the climate of the Ice Age, an adaptation that the remains discovered in Siberia, frozen and therefore almost intact, have made it possible to study in detail.

The Elephants of the North

Northern elephants had characteristics and organs that their cousins in warmer lands lacked entirely. Their fleece was made in three thicknesses: a dense underlayer, 4 to 6 inches (10–15 cm) thick, then the fur itself, and finally long external hairs (the "jarres"). The skin, which was almost an inch (2 cm) thick at the head, covered a large layer of fat.

The small size of the ears reduced the loss of heat. The trunk, also covered with hair, differed primarily in the two digits that it had on the end: Modern Asian elephants only have one, and those of African elephants are very small. The mammoths must therefore have been able to grasp plants with great delicateness and precision.

△ Mammoths from the Rouffignac cave (Dordogne), which contains more than 150 drawings of these animals, painted or carved over an area of more than one-half mile (700 m).

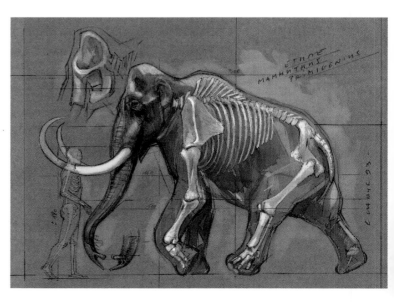

The long curved tusks, which often appear very worn, would have made it possible to sweep away snow. The feet rested on real cushions of skin, fibers, and fat that surrounded the toes. The animal must have been both well protected, very supple, and silent when walking. One important detail: The anus of mammoths was closed by a small pad that would come up against it, forming a valve.

Well Protected

The animal was also rather specialized in cold or cool areas. Appearing in Europe and in North Asia during the next-to-last glaciation, it blossomed during the last. But they had vanished from France 12,000 to 15,000 years ago. Had the environment become warmer? Probably. Or perhaps they had been overhunted by man? Possibly. For whatever reason, mammoths had already begun to move toward the north. They climbed further and further, and soon they were found only in Siberia and in the northernmost regions of Russia. It is believed that they survived for several millennia, until around 6,000 years before the present. The remains exhumed in Wrangel's Island, in the Arctic Ocean, however, have been dated at 1700 years before the present.

▶ ▶ ▶

A mother and her baby . . . .
It is believed that the shape
of the tusks made it
possible for the animals
to sweep away the snow
better. Some of the tusks
that have been found were
very worn at the end.

THE FIRST FROZEN MAMMOTH

Mammoths found intact in the ice or in the frozen mud had been described in Russia for a century when, in 1901, a scientific expedition succeeded in bringing one back, in pieces, in a refrigerator car. The first frozen mammoth had, however, been discovered by a Tunguz hunter in 1799, at the mouth of the Lena. This hunter had to wait four years before being able to extract the animal's enormous tusks, which he wanted from the frozen mud. An expedition then arrived to view the animal, but a bit too late: The flesh was decomposed and devoured, the mammoth gave off a horrible smell. It was the same throughout the nineteenth century. Scientists always arrived too late to view the decomposing animals.

But Siberia is big and, in August 1900, the news arrived that another mammoth had been dislodged by a rise in the river Bereskovka, almost at the eastern end of Siberia. A scientific expedition was dispatched. It left in May 1901, and arrived after almost five months of travel. A hut was built above the animal, which had been preserved by the cold—a fire had to be made to thaw it out. Then began the race against decomposition in order to cut apart the enormous cadaver and to package it in parts. The muscles were fresh, the stomach contained 33 pounds (15 kg) of plant matter. The animal had numerous fractures: It is believed to have fallen into a crevice.

The mammoth— we dreamed about it almost as much as the dinosaurs.

From the arrival in Europe of the Cro-Magnons to the end of the last glaciation, this European civilization lasted for at least 250 centuries.

F rom Spain as far as Ukraine and even as far as northeast Russia, from around 40,000 to 10,000 years ago, there was only one great civilization.

Never So Good

The "upper Paleolithic" European represents a real high point. Never, until that time, had stone been worked so well, had hunting been so good. Never had humans been so efficient. Much hunting was done in groups, and the great herds were exploited. At the end of this period, these hunters were even killing deer and horses in great numbers. They waited for them at river fords or trapped them in narrow valleys. In Petersfels, in Baden-Wurttemberg (southern Germany) the remains of 1,200 deer have been found—obviously killed in many hunts. At the same time, as with the objects, the images on the walls of caves had become splendid. Four major groups succeeded each other, with regional variations.

From the Change in Tools

First there was the Aurignacian and its tools, at the beginning still rather thick, its assegai points in bone, and its first painted figures: The paintings in the Chauvet cave (Ardeche, France) and the statuettes of the Swabian Jura (Germany), dated between 30,000 and 32,000 years, are already masterpieces. Then, in the Gravettian, very fine points were shaped, but most striking were fine, large dwellings constructed there, often partially dug in the ground. In Kostienki, a cluster of sites near Voronezh (Russia), diggers have found an area 119 feet (36 m) long and 59 feet (18 m) wide, with nine fireplaces aligned in the center and blocks around the perimeter. In Mezina and Mezhirich, in the Ukraine, massive huts were constructed with the bones of mammoths. In France, many huts built on a circle of large stones surrounding a hollowed-out area were constructed in Vigne-Brun near Roanne. And it was at this time that the famous statuettes of women, often buxom, were sculpted, which prehistorians have called "Venuses" after the Roman goddess of love.

Masterpieces of Mass Production

The Solutrean extended only from the north of Spain to the center of France. For tools, it marks the return to progressive shaping (in the style of bifaces). Alongside classic tools such as blades, chisels, and other scrapers, the masterpieces of Solutrean work are the "leaves" of flint, which are very fine and shaped blow by blow, in succession. It is also in this period, 20,000 years ago, that the oldest sewing needles and the first propelling devices made their appearance. But the strange Solutrean lasted only a few millennia—outside of its area, the Gravettian continued—before yielding to the Magdalenian. This was the period of mass production, of efficiency, of innumerable flint blades, of numerous camps at the north of rivers, of deer hunting that became a real specialty, of the caves at Lascaux, Niaux, and Altamira, of decorated harpoons, and of jewels. Images everywhere!

△ One of the most celebrated works of prehistory: the "hooded Venus" found at the beginning of the twentieth century in Brassempouy (Landes, France). Carved of ivory, it was made approximately 25,000 years ago.

Deer hunters, manufacturers of blades, builders of huts . . . and "artists," too.

25,000 YEARS OF HISTORY

The World also Changes

During 25,000 years, the climate often fluctuated from cold to less cold or to temperate. Around 35,000 years ago there was a significant, rather mild "interlude." The maximum cold appears to have been reached from 20,000 to 18,000 years ago. Then there was a slight warming that lasted approximately one thousand years, during which the caves of Lascaux were painted. The fluctuations then became more numerous and shorter, as if the climate did not know which way to jump . . . . Finally, around 9,500 years ago, several really temperate centuries saw the noticeable receding of the glaciers, and the trees multiplied . . . . It was then that the great European civilization of the High Paleolithic dissolved. It would survive for a time in northern areas where deer had taken refuge. More to the south, it would be necessary to adapt to another world: that of the forests.

THE BURIAL PLACES OF SUNGIR

In 1964, 93 miles (150 km) to the northeast of Moscow, three burial places were discovered dated at 20,000 to 23,000 years. Sungir man was laid out on his back, his head turned toward the northeast, his hands crossed on his chest. He had been covered with red ocher. Mixed in with his bones were 35,000 ivory pearls. They must have been sewn to his clothes—he may have been wearing a parka and pants—and woven through his hair. This man also wore jewelry made of deer teeth with a disc of perforated schist on his hair, a large necklace, and ivory bracelets. He was big, and he had died when he was between 55 and 65 years old. Less well preserved but equally rich, was a nearby burial place of a woman and, 10 feet (3 m) away, that of two children buried head to foot and covered with pearls, pendants, bracelets, and rings. Alongside of them were placed 16 ivory lances, one of which measured 8 feet (2.4 m) (!), as well as points and daggers, also in ivory.

▲ A Solutrean "laurel leaf paint." The purpose of such pieces is unknown. Were they spear points? Knives? Many of them are masterpieces of workmanship.

▲ An Aurignacian tool: the so-called "steep" scraper. This tool was specifically used for preparing skins.

▲ A Gravettian tool: the so-called "Noailles" burins. Burins, with their sturdy points, made it possible to cut, to make grooves, and to carve.

For throwing, hunting, and fishing weapons, propelling devices were invented approximately 20,000 years ago. They were often decorated, which proves the value attached to them. Here is a person using a Magdalenian spear thrower.

FINE BLADES, POINTS IN BONE, NEEDLES . . .

It took time, but finally we are there: Tens of thousands of years after the appearance of modern humans, the evolution of tools begins to accelerate.

1. First, they arrive with tools. But tools wear out and must be replaced. The people of the group know the area, of course, and know where to find flint of acceptable quality. They go there to select the blocks to be worked.

2. The block is first tested (it must "sound" well and therefore not have any cracks), then roughed out with the help of a strong hammer (a pebble). There's no need to carry the entire piece.

A Solutrean invention: the bone needle with an eye. Needles prove that sewing existed. But how was it done before?

3. Still using the hard hammer, the worker fashions the core, in order to be able to remove blades from it. The striking plan must be carefully prepared.

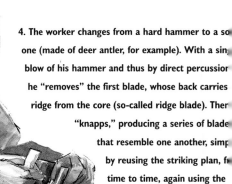

4. The worker changes from a hard hammer to a so[ft] one (made of deer antler, for example). With a sin[gle] blow of his hammer and thus by direct percussion[,] he "removes" the first blade, whose back carries [a] ridge from the core (so-called ridge blade). The[n he] "knapps," producing a series of blade[s] that resemble one another, simp[ly] by reusing the striking plan, f[rom] time to time, again using the hard hammer.

S tone tools became finer and could be mass produced. This appeared first in points made of bone and in what are known as "batons": long instruments made of deer antlers equipped with a hole that could be used (the edges are polished, worn). Used for what purpose? Perhaps for emergency repairs.

The Blow of the Harpoon

Then came the needle made of bone that, with its eye, proves that these people knew about sewing. With what thread? Perhaps with animal tendons, particularly from deer. Contemporary with the needle, the propelling device was a kind of lever, a hunting weapon that made it possible to throw the assegai spear with greater force. Finally, the harpoon was invented, with its points (barbs) on the side and a hole through which a cord was threaded: an ingenious invention that made it possible to launch a weapon and to embed it in the game without letting it go, while remaining at a distance.

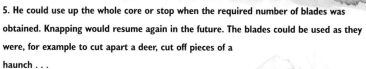

5. He could use up the whole core or stop when the required number of blades was obtained. Knapping would resume again in the future. The blades could be used as they were, for example to cut apart a deer, cut off pieces of a haunch . . .

6. Often, the blades were altered to form a specific tool. Here a blade has been modified on one end to produce a scraper, recognizable by its rather thick "snout." Scrapers were specifically used to work on skins, but they could also scrape wood and bone.

7. Another very important tool, the burin, was obtained using a special technique: The "blow of the burin" was made on one end of the blade in such a way as to create a point that was both sharp and solid. Burins seemed to have been specifically used to work on bone. In the future, they would be used on everything: bone, wood, skins, shells . . .

Work, a long time ago.

8. The work completed, the tools were put down. They were taken and reworked if the raw material was not abundant. Or others would be made from them. It seems that some tools would be left at the site where the work was done. And many would be left behind when it became necessary to move camp to reach another stop on the annual migration.

Having begun in the nineteenth century, the sensational discoveries of prehistoric art have not stopped. Everything indicates that they are likely to continue.

THE DISCOVERY OF PREHISTORIC ART

I t is in part because of an image that the reality of prehistory was accepted in the nineteenth century. In fact, in 1864, in the shelter of La Madeleine, on the banks of the Vézère (Dordogne), the discovery was made of a beautiful image of a mammoth engraved on a shoulder blade . . . apparently when the bone was still fresh. This proved definitively that humans had truly lived at the same time as these renowned extinct animals. They had seen them and drawn them.

A Wall of Incredulity

Nevertheless, people had difficulty accepting some of the images, such as the paintings on the walls of caves—art known as "Rupestrian." In 1879, a little girl looked up in the cave of Altamira, in Spain, where her father was excavating. She saw a ceiling covered with bison, some red, some black—now famous. But when her father made the discovery public, he was considered a forger. For more than twenty years, no one wanted to believe that prehistoric humans were capable of painting the masterpieces in the caves.

On All Continents

But that they were able to do so had to be accepted in the face of the large number of discoveries that came about because of the passion for prehistory. Decorated caves or shelters were found by the dozens, first in the north of Spain and the south of France, then on other continents. Prehistoric images exist in northern Africa, in the Sahara (in Tassili, Akakus, Air, Atlas, Fezzan . . .), in South Africa, in South America (specifically in Brazil and Argentina), and in North America (Mexico, the United States). The image also proliferated among the aborigines of Australia. There are decorated caves in India, carvings on the rocks of Central Asia . . . . In Zimbabwe, in southeast Africa, more than 300 sites of paintings have been studied, of which the oldest appears to date back 13,000 years. It is probable that, in one form or another, all of the populations of the world have "made" images.

Some Remain to Be Discovered

Given the amount of time that has passed since this research began, it might seem that all prehistoric images, all those that survived, are known. This is not so. More are found every year! A number of discoveries were made at the Apollo XI cave in Zimbabwe; the great shelter of Pedra Furada in Brazil; the rock carvings of Central Asia; numerous decorated caves in India; in France, the Cosquer cave near Marseille, which can only be reached by diving 135 feet (40 m) down and climbing into a flooded gallery, and the Chauvet cave in Ardeche. In Portugal, the carvings of Foz Coa extend for several miles.

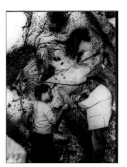

▲ Carving of an animal on an ivory blade.

▲ Abbé Henri Breuil (1879–1961), the great French prehistorian, at work in the Lascaux cave.

The Great Cave of Arcy-sur-Cure (France) is an original: People had been visiting it for centuries, and no one had seen anything . . . . This mammoth became visible after a portion of the wall was cleaned in 1997.

▲ ▲ ▲

Prehistoric paintings exist in India as they do elsewhere. In the State of Madhya Pradesh (India), in the Jihri shelter no. 7, there are representations from various eras, from prehistory to historic times.

A carved mammoth proved part of prehistory.

The Reign of the Image?

What remains to us of prehistoric art is perhaps only a minuscule part of what was painted, sculpted, or carved 10,000, 20,000, or 30,000 years ago. It is even possible that the majority of images have disappeared: If this is the case, we can tell ourselves that the humans of those times, and throughout the world, lived all of their lives amidst images, stories, and beliefs that these images created. Do human societies need images as much as they need food to survive?

Well-hidden Treasures

Modern techniques make it possible occasionally to discover images that were not visible at first. In the Great Cave of Arcy-sur-Cure, in Burgundy (France), more than a hundred figures covered with accumulations or almost erased were made visible using infrared, ultraviolet, and computer-processed photography. None of the many visitors to this cave, over the years, had noted any images. Today it is one of the principal decorated caves in France. The future may hold still more discoveries.

MYSTERIOUS SYMBOLS

Why was there painted, in Lascaux, a rectangle and a dotted line on the head of a great stag? In Pech-Merle, in the Quercy, many dotted lines mark the ceiling of a passage. Almost everywhere, on the images or next to them, on objects also, prehistoric artists have traced symbols. A cave such as Niaux, in the Pyrenees, contains more than 300 symbols. In some caves, such as Altamira, in Spain, there are even walls that contain nothing else. The symbols fall into categories—dots, dashes, "barbs"—with regional preferences: Tectiforms (in the shape of a roof) are numerous in the Perigord, for example. Although some can occasionally be interpreted as weapons (for example, the barbs that are seen on or near animals), the meaning of the symbols is generally as enigmatic, if not more so, than that of the figures.

THE TRACES OF RUPESTRIAN ART THROUGHOUT THE WORLD

Sites of rupestrian art: In the form of carvings, paintings, or sculptures, these sites have been discovered on all continents.

THE FIRST GREAT ART OF EUROPE

For more than two hundred centuries, from Portugal to Russia, people have drawn, painted, carved, sculpted. A matter of religion, perhaps, but what else?

The first art of Europe lasted more than 20,000 years. It appears to have exploded shortly after the arrival of the Cro-Magnons, with masterpieces such as the animals in the Chauvet cave and the statuettes of the Swabian Jura, and lasted until the end of the Magdalenian era, approximately 10,000 years before the modern era.

A Multiplication of Images

For more than two hundred centuries, much indecipherable scribbling was produced along with masterpieces. Hands applied paint on walls and threw the paint around. To draw, paint, or model, the artist disappeared into the deepest part of some caves, hundreds of feet away from the light of day. Walls were carved in entire panels, tablets of stone in the hundreds. Symbols multiplied. And marvelous animals were carved in bone or in ivory.

The Time of Hands, of Figurines

Today more than three hundred decorated caves are known throughout Europe. However, the history of this art cannot be told. All that is possible is to place some reference points, thanks to dating that has been done, both on paintings and on sculpted or decorated objects (so-called "mobile" art). Thus, following the early successes that date back to more than 30,000 years, around 25,000 or 27,000 years ago a period began in which many hands were drawn. Most often, these were hands that were applied on walls and around which paint had been thrown. They appear in negative, as in the Cosquer, Gargas, and Arcy-sur-Cure (France) caves. This was followed by the great period of the "Venus," female figurines that have been found in Brassempouy and Lespugue (France); in Willendorf (Austria), in Avdeevo and Kostienki (Russia), and even in Malta (Siberia).

Hundreds of Tablets

And there was more. A great period of painting began around 20,000 years ago with the figures in the Cosquer cave and

The figure known as the "jumping cow" in Lascaux. Note the consistent procedure of rotating the left hind leg to make it come out again on the abdomen. Other remarkable elements: the symbols in front of the animal and the small horses that are passing in the opposite direction.

the complete masterpiece that is the Lascaux cave (approximately 17,000 years ago). Finally, art reached the Pyrenees and the Cantabrian region (the Altamira paintings are between 15,400 and 13,500 years old; those of Niaux, between 13,800 and 12,800). This was also the golden age of carved and chiseled objects. The German site of Gonnersdorf, in the Rhine Valley, dated at 12,600 years, contains approximately four hundred stone tablets: horses, primarily (and some other animals), but also stylized silhouettes of women. The Enlène cave (14,000–13,000 years old), in the Pyrenees, contains more than eight hundred carved tablets.

Why These Images?

What do these paintings represent? Animals, of course. In many of the caves, it is the relationship between bison-horse or aurochs-horse that predominates (Lascaux and Altamira). In others, there are more mammoths (Rouffignac), rhinoceros, and cats (Chauvet, Arcy-cur-Cure). Symbols are everywhere (dots, sticks, arrows . . .). But although a particular configuration appears frequently, the meaning of these figures and these groupings remains unknown. During the nineteenth century, it was said that prehistoric painters worked solely for the love of art. Then they were inspired by the magic of the hunt, then to show the association between feminine and masculine symbols.

And Today?

The majority of prehistorians today refuse to interpret. Some, however, speak of the spirit and methods of shamanism, based on communication with spirits of nature and on the trance: This is seen among the hunting peoples of Siberia and suggested in the art of the Bushmen of South Africa. Religion is obviously behind this world of images. But it has also been noted that the decoration of some caves changed over time, that the figures and even the groupings had been completed, reworked, corrected, sometimes at intervals of thousands of years. The beliefs also could have changed . . .

A beautiful piece of European prehistory: the bone "object" found in the Bruniquel cave (Tarn, France), sculpted in the shape of a bounding horse. It dates from approximately 15,000 years ago.

To the deepest of caves . . .

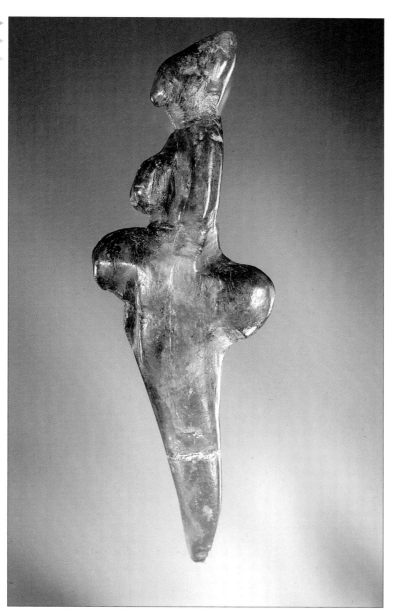

One of the celebrated "Venus" figurines. This one was discovered at the beginning of the twentieth century in the Grimaldi caves, in Italy. It has been named "Polichinelle" because of its humps . . . . The majority of female statuettes from the same period (from 20,000 to 25,000 years ago) have exaggerated shapes.

AN IMPORTANT INVENTION IN JAPAN

Fascinating Japan: During prehistory as during history, it experienced long periods of little change and others in which it was in advance of the entire world.

During the last glaciation, from 90,000 to 100,000 years before the modern era, eastern Asia had changed perhaps even more than western Europe. Siberia extended in the direction of North America via the Bering plain, more than 620 miles (1,000 km) wide. The Indochinese peninsula was connected to Indonesia. These vast expanses that had previously emerged (800,000 sq. mi. or 2 million sq. km), were known as the continent of Sunda.

A Prehistory Engulfed

When the level of the seas climbed after the glaciation, they submerged enormous expanses that humans had frequented for millennia. The earlier plains and coastal areas were often the easiest to inhabit, the richest in resources. Thus, most likely what the rising seas engulfed was the most interesting part of Asian prehistory. This explains certain research problems: In Japan, a country of accidental geology whose landscape has been completely changed by the activity of earthquakes and glaciations, few human remains have been preserved.

Behind . . .

Japanese prehistoric sites, nevertheless, number in the dozens. Four technical periods have been identified, the oldest of which was based on shaped pebbles and fragments—and even bifaces, which are rare in this part of the world. The oldest identified site, Sozudai on the island of Kyushu (in the south), dates back at least 70,000 years. There are traces of occupation at 150,000 years. But Korea and China have sites that are much older, and the Japanese sites of *Homo erectus* from those times may have disappeared with Earth's upheavals. During a second period, between 20,000 and 15,000 years ago, well-formed blades appeared. Tools or parts of tools then became smaller (microliths). In short, Japan followed the same technical evolution as the rest of the world with, however, some delay in stone tools.

. . . and Suddenly Ahead

But then, a remarkable technical advance took place on the archipelago. It was, in fact, in the south of Japan, still on the island of Kyushu, that some of the oldest, if not the oldest, pottery in the world first made its appearance. This took place between 12,000 and 10,000 before the modern era. Pottery is generally linked with the world of peasants; however, here, at the Fukui site, for example, it appeared thousand of years before any trace of agriculture. This activity was invented by people who were collectors, fishermen, and hunters.

Potters and Fishermen

This pottery is known as Jômon because it was decorated by means of impressions of ropes (jômon doki). Its creators gathered, collected—roots, grain plants (buckwheat and millet)—and they also fished. They even practiced deep sea fishing beginning 9,000 or 8,000 years before the modern era, another achievement. They accomplished crossings of 31 miles (50 km) to

The Jômon pottery of Japan was neither painted nor made on a potter's wheel. It underwent many stages: conical bases, flat bases, vases with protuberances, increasingly complicated forms, and finally vases imitating Chinese bronzes—several thousand years ahead ▼ at the beginning, ▼ several thousand years ▼ behind at the end!

THE PALEOLITHIC SITES OF JAPAN

Modern coasts

HOKKAIDO

KOREA

Coasts
20,000 years ago

HONSHU

OCEAN

Fukui

Sozudai

KYUSHU

PACIFIC

● Paleolithic sites
○ Jômon sites

The Ainu were, it is thought, a people indigenous to Japan. Pushed back from the south and the center, today they live only in the north (Hokkaido, Kuriles, south of Sakhalin peninsula). Possible inventors of Jômon pottery 12,000 years ago, today they are attempting to preserve some of their traditions.

When the Japanese did not need to become peasants.

THE ENIGMA OF BAMBOO

Almost everywhere in East Asia, the working of stone appears to have been less advanced than in the rest of the Old World. The use of simple worked pebbles seems to have lasted longer there, bifaces remaining rare and of late vintage. What happened? In the Far East grows an all-purpose plant: bamboo. Not only are its shoots a food source, but the structure and quality of its wood made it possible to create excellent tools: extraordinarily sharp points, knives that cut like steel, efficient chisels . . . daggers, farming tools, combs, containers. They had no need to go in search of heavy blocks of stone that were difficult to work.

supply themselves with obsidian (a volcanic glass from which marvelous tools were made), and Jômon pottery has been found on the island of Okinawa. They lived in small villages in dwellings that were partially underground, and perhaps permanent: There were enough resources and variety that they no longer needed to move during the year. There were abundant piles of shells . . . . The Japanese would thus have been among the inventors of the sedentary dwelling. But this culture, which would last more than 10,000 years, would not adopt agriculture until much later, long after China. On this point, Japan would again be behind. It should be noted that the abundant resources of the archipelago were capable of feeding an already numerous non-peasant population.

To have an idea of the landscape in which the people of prehistoric Japan evolved, one must travel far . . . . Here, in a crater, is a lake on the island of Hokkaido, the large island at the north of the archipelago.

THE SAHARA OF THE HIPPOPOTAMUS

It rained in the Sahara–enough so that waterfalls were born in the mountains and formed rivers. This was, 8,000 or 10,000 years ago, the Sahara of great lakes, of hippopotamus and fisherman.

Fluctuations in climate did not spare Western Africa. But instead of passing from temperate to cold and back again, the climate there was always balanced between the dry and the humid, or, more precisely, between much and little desert.

Mousterian and Aterian

Some periods of prehistory were more humid there: The people who made the Acheulian tools lived there and, after them, the people of the Mousterian, exactly as in the Near East and in Europe. From a cultural point of view, the Sahara and Northern Africa were one. The uniformity remained as, little by little, the Mousterian modernized and gave rise to lighter pieces of the Aterian around 40,000 to 30,000 years before the modern era. Then the climate became arid. It was the period when, in Europe, the ice reached its maximum extension. The Sahara thus became a desert.

A Cooler Climate

The Sahara remained dry for between 20,000 and 10,000 years, when populations similar to the Cro-Magnon in Europe lived in northern Africa and

fashioned very thin blades from very small cores. They evolved in a Mediterranean landscape and in a cooler climate than now: There were cedars near Algiers. These "Iberomaurusians" saw gazelles, antelopes and gnus, horses and asses, stags and even great megaceros stags. They had to avoid getting too close to lions, panthers, and bears. The inhabitants of the Taforalt cave near Oujda, in Morocco, wore pendants of stone and pierced shells: They did some carving. In this cave the remains of 185 individuals have been found, among them 100 children.

▲ In the Djanet region, near
▲ modern Tassili (Algeria).

Between much and little desert.

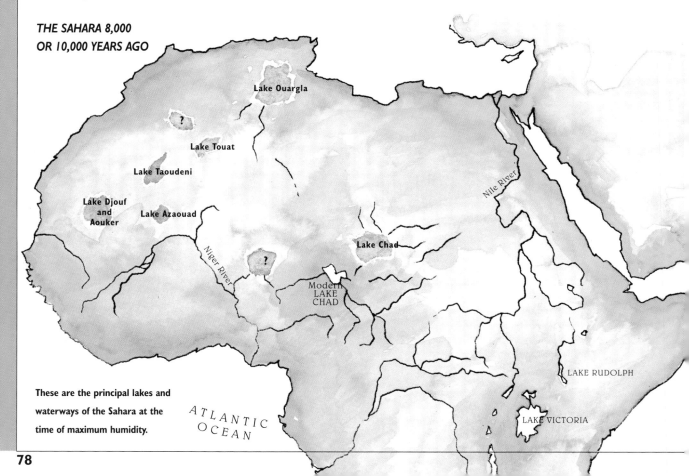

THE SAHARA 8,000 OR 10,000 YEARS AGO

Lake Ouargla

?

Lake Touat

Lake Taoudeni

Lake Djouf and Aouker

Lake Azaouad

Niger River

?

Lake Chad

Modern LAKE CHAD

Nile River

LAKE RUDOLPH

LAKE VICTORIA

ATLANTIC OCEAN

These are the principal lakes and waterways of the Sahara at the time of maximum humidity.

The Land of Great Lakes

Life returned to the Sahara toward the end of the ice age. Basically, life is water. The great lakes of the Sahara returned. The deposits they left are proof. Seven or eight great lakes at least—some forming small interior seas—were found from southern Algeria as far as Chad. Lake Chad itself was enormous, several times greater than its current miserable 9,600 square miles (25,000 km²), and emptied into another, even larger, lake. These lakes were fed by waterways originating in the great mountainous massifs: Hoggar, Air, Tassili, Tibesti. Three of them gave rise to the rivers that, in turn, cause the Niger to swell.

What Water!

It is no surprise if, under these conditions, geologists and prehistorians discover the remains of aquatic animals in the middle of the Sahara: fish and mollusks, tortoise, hippopotamus, or crocodiles. The shores of these great lakes must have been covered with enough vegetation for giraffes, buffalo, rhinoceros, and elephants to prosper there. All are powerful consumers: An elephant in captivity eats approximately 450 pounds (200 kg) of hay per day . . . and drinks more than 54 gallons (200 l) of water.

Fishing Villages

There were people who lived mainly by fishing: Thousands of harpoons and bone hooks are proof. These encampments or villages of fishermen are found from Mauritania as far as the Nile. It is certain that in those times, the type of vegetation that currently grows in countries such as Mali or Niger then grew much further north. But there was no "green Sahara," as was originally believed. Large green beaches extended around lakes; green corridors ran the length of the waterways. But elsewhere, aridity maintained its hold, always ready to advance, as has since taken place.

ARTISTS OF THE SAHARA

Other evidence of the human presence were the figures left on innumerable walls, in the shelters of Tassili (Algerian Sahara), and in other massifs: Akakus, Air, Adrar, Saharan Atlas . . . . There are carvings and paintings, some paintings that first were carved. The oldest may date beyond the tenth millennium. The art of hunters shows animals, obviously wild, specifically the large humped antelopes known as bubals, but also hippopotamus, elephants . . . . The paintings known as "round heads," so called because the humans, who are numerous, have heads in the shape of disks, are also very old, and rank as some of the most beautiful in prehistory. The precise chronology of these works is still subject to discussion. Among the carvings, those of the Djerat wadi have been found at seventy-five sites over 22 miles (35 km).

Fragment of a painting from Tassili (Algeria) showing a giraffe. On the walls of the Ti-n-Touloult site, near Djerat, one measures 28 feet (8.5 m). In addition to giraffes, there are many elephants and rhinoceros, evidence that these large animals must have been able to find food.

THOSE WHO INVENTED THE INDIANS OF AMERICA

Paleoindians, hunters of mammoths and giant bison in the Great Plains. Archaic Indians who were both fishermen and builders as far as Labrador, inhabitants of a desert with their sandals and their baskets: The origins of modern Indians go back a long time.

There was a time when America did not have a prehistory; it was the complete "New World." Then, in 1926, a finely worked point was found right next to the skeleton of a bison, in the layer of earth surrounding one side. The bison belonged to an extinct species; it was very large, and the point must have been used to kill it. This discovery was in Folsom, New Mexico. Today, the Folsom sites reflect a culture dated at approximately 9,000 to 8,000 years before the modern era, that is, one that preceded, and perhaps may even have invented, the Indians of America: This was the world of the Paleoindians.

In Order to Kill Large Beasts

These points were weapons. The two long striations on both sides must have made it possible to better attach them to the end of an assegai. Older by approximately a millennium are the points of Clovis (another New Mexican site), which exhibit smaller striations. Both obviously indicate that hunting peoples lived there. At many sites, in fact, the remains of animals have been found mixed with these points.

Sites and Specialized Tools

These hunting sites are located mainly in the Great Plains of the United States. At the oldest, a single large animal was killed: a large bison, a mastodon, a mammoth (different from those in Europe), or even a giant antelope, a musk ox.... The sites with projectile points are often specialized: There are some where only wood was cut. Some show evidence of a very short occupation, while others show that the hunters stayed for almost an entire season. In the most recent sites, entire herds were tracked.

Hunters pushed the animals toward the top of a cliff or into a cul-de-sac. In

Modern bison in the prairies of the American West.

Hunters lying in wait somewhere in the North American Plains, perhaps 10,000 years ago.

Casper, Wyoming, they also pushed a herd of ancient great bison into an area of dunes where the animals became stuck. Then the massacre began, but only of animals between the ages of six months and two-and-one-half years. Had there been selection? At another site, the skeletons of approximately two hundred bison were found.

Changing Way of Life

Ten thousand years before the modern era, the great North American glacier still extended as far as Lake Superior, Lake Huron, and the Saint Lawrence River. Its progressive retreat had two important results for humans: It freed up territory and it allowed the forest to expand. Some groups adapted to the temperate forest environment. They obviously had to change their way of life completely, using more diverse resources—fishing and gathering more—adapting, in short, to this "new world" of trees. The tools for cutting wood multiplied (axes, adzes, and gouges of polished stone), as well as the net weights for fishing. They still hunted, of course: stag, beaver, raccoon . . .

Large Houses

Along the coasts, other groups were more specialized in their exploitation of the sea: They invented the movable harpoon

head before the Paleoinuit. It was during this period (7,000 to 8,000 years ago) and in this region (from Labrador to New England) that some of the oldest known houses in America have been dated. Built on the Labrador coast, by the ocean, they include some very long structures that could have housed several families. One of them measured 264 feet (80 m) long. These people, moreover, went as far as the Arctic.

The Cultures of the Desert

In the western United States, from New Mexico to the California coast, groups of points have been found without striations. The hunters from the desert cultures cut extremely fine pieces in obsidian. This dark, translucent volcanic rock is an ideal material. The dryness of the climate favored preserving tools made of bone or wood, and even basketry: Stone was not everything. Further to the south, in Mexico, desert conditions made it possible to find objects made of twisted fibers: baskets, cords, sandals. Approximately 6,000 to 5,000 years before the modern era, and still in Mexico, in the tradition of the desert, people lived by gathering grasses, cactus, agave, reptiles, and insects. Familiar with bow and arrow, they also hunted small mammals and birds.

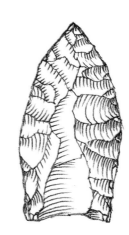

The points of Clovis and of Folsom, classic pieces of American prehistory.

AND THE WOMEN?
If it is agreed that the Paleoindian cultures lived by hunting, the same was not true of the cultures of the forest and the desert. Here, gathering played an important role. But this is a traditionally female task; that is, most of the food was provided by women. This was probably true in the Southwest United States and in Mexico. Among the Tohono O'Odahm Indians in the northwest of Mexico, who have preserved the culture of the desert and do not farm, women provide three-quarters of the food. This is thought to have been the case in the so-called "hunting" cultures, such as in Australia, where studies of aboriginal life have shown that most of the food is also provided by women.

THE PEOPLE
OF THE GREAT NORTH

Ten thousand years before the modern era, what parts of the world remained to be populated? The Antarctic would still wait for a long time. The last islands of the Pacific–Easter Island, Hawaii, New Zealand–would not be reached until between 500 and 800 years before the modern era. Only the American Great North remained.

Approximately ten thousand years before the modern era, from northern Siberia to Greenland, groups of humans learned to live in the Great North, that is, on frozen ground, under the snow, even on ice fields, at latitudes where it is night for months at a time.

Across Beringia

These are formidable places. The adventure began in Siberia. People lived there 10,000 years ago as they had in central Europe or in western Europe 5,000 years earlier. Groups slowly followed the great glacier of the north on its slow retreat. As they naturally followed the movement of animals, some also lived in "Beringia" (that is, the Bering Strait when the lowering of the seas resulted in its emergence during the glaciations). Even in their period of greatest expansion, glaciers never completely covered Alaska. With their retreat, enormous spaces opened up toward the east. It became possible to follow the caribou (Canadian deer) and musk ox.

Seal hunt on the ice field. Human adaptation to life in the frozen regions was slower and developed last. The people who lived during the time of the glaciations did not travel to neighboring areas of glaciers, which could not support any life.

From Siberia to Greenland

But since resources became rarer as people approached less hospitable areas, these landsmen also had to learn to exploit, or better exploit, the sea. On an island in the Aleutian archipelago called Anangula, then probably connected to the continent, a community of fishermen lived, 7,000 to 10,000 years ago, in houses that were half-buried, for which the entrance was probably through the roof. The community used tools reminiscent of those of both Siberia and Japan . . . . They were also found in the north of Alaska. The adventure of the Great North had begun.

Toward Baffin Island

Four to five thousand years ago, cultures appeared that have been grouped together under the name "Paleoeskimo" or "Paleoinuit." From Alaska, they spread out rapidly to the east: 3,000 miles (5,000 km) in two or three centuries. They reached the Canadian Arctic, Baffin and Ellesmere Islands, Labrador, and even Greenland. The culture of Dorset, named

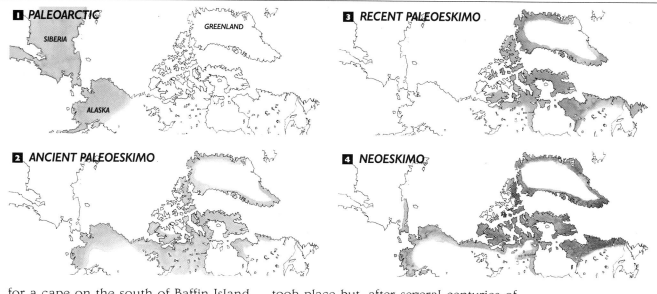

1 PALEOARCTIC

SIBERIA

GREENLAND

ALASKA

3 RECENT PALEOESKIMO

2 ANCIENT PALEOESKIMO

4 NEOESKIMO

The harsh apprentice-ship of the Arctic.

◁ From Siberia to Greenland:

◁ the great theater of

◁ adaptation to polar life.

for a cape on the south of Baffin Island, where a fur trading post was established, belongs to these cultures.

A House for One Hundred People

The Dorsetians lived for almost two thousand years from Labrador to as far as the most extreme Arctic deserts (from Banks Island to Greenland). They were thus perfectly adapted. With good tools made of very small stones developed from earlier Siberian and Alaskan cultures, they lived from the sea, where they hunted seals and walrus (but also caribou on land). Among the most original of their developments are the houses in which they came together at certain times of the year, perhaps in autumn, the season of greatest abundance. Perhaps this was the holiday season. These houses reached 135 feet (40 m) in length, and an estimated one hundred people could live in one. They were covered with skins. Then the groups would disperse to face the winter. Perhaps they had skis. Perhaps they already built igloos?

Following the Whales

Modern inhabitants of the Great North are not descendants of the Dorsetians, but of a group of cultures from the Arctic Ocean coast in Alaska. These people had developed sea fishing and even whale hunting. They had kayaks and umiaks. At first, these "Neoeskimos" still lived in the old half-buried houses constructed from stone, peat, and whalebone. They made tools and weapons from polished slate, bone, and ivory. As they followed the migrating whales, they got as far as Greenland before the year 1000. With the climate becoming colder beginning in the fourteenth century, they would abandon the cetaceans and adopt a way of life similar to that of the Dorsetians, with whom they apparently had hardly any interaction. Little is known about what

took place but, after several centuries of coexistence, by the fourteenth century the Dorsetians had disappeared from the central Arctic; by the sixteenth century they had disappeared from other areas. The Neoeskimos, by the intermediary of the Thule culture, are alone in having given birth to the recent cultures of the Great North.

Modern Kallaalits (and not Eskimos) of Greenland:
Two thousand years were required for humans,
leaving Siberia and passing through Alaska, to adapt
to life in the polar regions. ▽ ▽ ▽

ONE WORD FOR ANOTHER

Do not speak of Eskimos to indicate the modern peoples. The current inhabitants of the Arctic do not want this name. In Canada and in the north of Alaska the name is Inuit (which means humans); in the south of Alaska and in Siberia it is Yuit; finally, in Greenland it is Kallaalit. These are three different populations. The term Eskimo is used to describe several peoples and was, in fact, given by the Europeans. It is derived from Ayaskimew, an Indian word meaning "those who speak a foreign language." It should only be used to describe cultures from the past, such as those of the Paleoeskimos and the Neoeskimos, which themselves cover various groups.

1 Lake Mungo
2 Willandra Lakes

THE LONG MEMORY OF THE ABORIGINES

One of the most recent works in the "prehistoric" style, painted in Australia in 1964 at Nourlangie Rock. Its creator, Najobolmi, has painted more than 600 figures in forty-six shelters. These are not mythical creatures. The author wished to symbolize (and provoke?) the renaissance of his people. A large woman is lying on top of a man together with a Barramundi fish, a giant perch that lives in estuaries, both symbols of fertility. This painting is in the "radiographic" style: Internal organs are represented here.

In Australia, prehistorians have discovered very old human remains, paintings that are perhaps the oldest the world, a prehistory of which some memories are apparently retained in the myths of the Aborigines.

On the strangest continent of the world, the flattest, the driest, a most astonishing prehistory developed. It is the most vivid and the most current: 200,000 Australians, known as Aborigines, keep it in their memory, sometimes in their gestures. On the same rocky surfaces bearing figures that are 20,000 years old or more, can be seen representations of the boats and the guns of the British of the last century. The rupestrian art of Australia is both one of the oldest in the world, perhaps the oldest, and the most modern prehistoric art: There are paintings from the 1960s and some keepers of the sites are still painting now.

As did those of Europe, the prehistoric artists of Australia pressed their hands against the walls and threw the paint around them. These "negative" hands are located in Cathedral cave (Queensland).

Good Big Tools

After the first people landed at least 50,000 years ago, they must have first populated the coasts. There are sites in the southeast and the southwest that are 40,000 years old. As for the arid heart of Australia, people lived there at least 30,000 years ago. From these ancient times remain carvings, paintings, and rather clumsy big tools. In the north, around 20,000 years ago, inhabitants used axes that were remarkably sharp tools with a strange shape that may indicate that their users knew about handles. Nevertheless, for thousands of years, stone implements were basically small scrapers and large cutting tools for cutting wood or bone. This was how it was on the shores of the Willandra lakes, a series of dried-up lakes in New South Wales, and particularly on the shores of Mungo Lake, investigators found human remains 28,000 and 13,000 years old in a fossil dune. In fact, these crude tools reflect poorly the life they led.

Life at Mungo Lake

The rivermen lived mostly from the lake. The remains of numerous fish have been identified: 22,000 to 26,000 years ago, seven out of ten fish caught were perch.

giant kangaroos . . . . Curiously, these species disappeared everywhere shortly after the arrival of humans. In Cuddie Springs, in New South Wales, the bones of these animals were found with tools, some of which bore traces of blood. Analysis showed the DNA from this blood to be the same as that of the bones. And this was before the boomerang, the astonishing invention that dates back 10,000 years.

Kangaroo at the Nourlangie Rock site (Kakadu National Park, Northern Territory).

Their size is very similar within each site. They were apparently caught using nets in some places, hoop nets in others. In the nineteenth century, Aborigines on the banks of the Darling River fished using nets 330 feet (100 m) long made of plant fibers. Some sites at Mungo Lake, one of which has been dated at 32,000 years, give evidence of a single and unique meal, not without originality: At one, only frogs were killed; at another, 500 crayfish were consumed!

Too Efficient?

Life could, therefore, have been good, as archeology and ethnology have so demonstrated. Perhaps this good life was due in large part to the women who, in gathering, collecting, and killing the "small beasts," provided 75 percent of the food . . . . But hunting was also profitable. Perhaps these early inhabitants even hunted too much. When humans arrived in Australia, existing fauna included the diprotodon, a marsupial herbivore that may have weighed almost two tons,

THE "DREAM TIME"

All of Australia is marked with symbols. From the most ancient times, its inhabitants have painted. They have also carved. Deep in the galleries of the Koonalda cave, in the southern desert, where they came to extract flint, are hundreds of tracings made with fingers on tender walls: They are more than 20,000 years old. This was not a game. In fact, all of the rocky areas of Australia are marked. They bear witness to what the Aborigines themselves, in their tales, call the "dream time": the ancient times, the beginnings. The inhabitants of an area can say which way a being from these mythical times passed, where he slept, ate, what became of him . . . . And their tales seem to recall the beginnings, the time when they arrived via the sea, when the sea rose to cover immense areas—a memory 10,000 or 60,000 years old.

Here are some of the remarks made by Paddy Neowarra, of the Galerungary clan, representing the Ngarinyins (Kimberley, Australia) to prehistorians meeting at UNESCO on June 16, 1997: "The reason why we have come to you is because you are professionals in your own field of rupestrian art. We are the professionals of our own images. Our paintings are ours. It is our earthly Right. If we lose our Right, the paintings are empty. Our paintings are our life because Unggudd and the earth and the people are all connected to each other. [. . .] Archaeologists think about life in the past, we think about our living country. If we combine our knowledge, we can protect the art, the life, the country and the law. [. . .] We are the people that possessed the history and the feelings of down under. You, you have a unique point of view, a scientific point of view, but we can think reciprocally; you are the neighbors from above, we are the neighbors from down under. We move together, in friendship, in the wunan, each connected to the others."

THE DAWN OF ANOTHER WORLD

Ten to twelve thousand years ago, prehistory reached a threshold. Of course, it appears to have continued without change in many places. Nevertheless, in some areas, a radical change took place. Predators until then, humans were to become producers.

The Mureybet site, on the banks of the Euphrates (Syria). Today, submerged behind a dam, it contains the remains of one of the first villages and evidence of the first agricultural activities.

A t that time, the people of the North began to reach the Great North. Those in Europe saw the deer disappear and the temperatures become warmer. In Africa, the Sahara once again became somewhat green on the shores of revived rivers. It had rained. In North America, hunters with projectile points mastered the plains. Prehistory evolved while perpetuating itself: People were still hunters, fishermen, gatherers . . . . Yet in many regions of the world, this millennial way of life, which appeared to have reached its peak, also began to turn into "something else." Why would everything, or almost everything, change?

A Complete Success

A profound change was about to take place. In the Near East, from Palestine to the Euphrates, a civilization spread that was remarkable in that it was better able to exploit its environment, to make the maximum use of resources available. These were the natoufians, who hunted, fished, and harvested as many plants as possible, particularly wild grasses. They were so efficient and succeeded so well that they no longer needed to move with the seasons. It was possible to live in the same place year-round, in all weather.

Model of a house from the first village of Mureybet: circular, partially built into the ground.

One of the female statuettes found in Mureybet on the level that precedes the first evidence of agriculture.

First Villages

So huts or tents were abandoned. Houses were built, round ones, of earth and clay. The first villages appeared on the banks of the Euphrates, in the area of Damascus, in the Jordan Valley, 12,000 years before the modern era. It was in these areas that one or two thousand years later, at the end of changes that remain little understood, another way of life was invented: agriculture, what we call production. The grasses that were collected—wild wheat and barley—were selected, sown, grown. Precisely how this came about remains unknown, but it entailed a genuine revolution in human history.

In Latin America, Too

Other developments took place a short time later in Latin America. On the shores of the Pacific, from Ecuador to Chile, fishing resources were so abundant and sufficiently well exploited that other villages, other permanent establishments, were created. This took place approximately 10,000 years before the modern era. At the same time, strange innovations were taking place among the hunter-gatherers of the Andes: Wild plants were, little by little, becoming domesticated, cultivated. The inhabitants of the Guitarrero cave in Peru grew peppers and two kinds of beans beginning 8,000 years before the modern era, and corn two thousand years later. Several thousand years later, the arrival of these practices in North American coastal villages would create the first peasant civilizations there. An original evolution toward agriculture also occurred in Mexico.

To Each Its Inventions

And elsewhere? China, Southeast Asia, and India struggle to domesticate rice. Another original invention took place in New Guinea. On this large island, which always seemed to lag behind the rest of the world, 6,000 years ago or more, the inhabitants developed sugar cane culture and the production of bananas . . . . Perhaps the inhabitants of the Nile Valley and the Sahara were also innovators. What is astonishing is to see all of these inventions occur independently within a period of thousands of years, a rather short time on the scale of prehistory. It was as if the societies of hunters-fishermen-gatherers, arriving at their maximum productivity in favorable environments, naturally moved on to other things, entering into this other world, that of peasants.

A MATTER OF RELIGION?

To explain how the revolution in agriculture (and also that of husbandry) could have occurred, researchers cite changes of climate and population growth. The French prehistorian Jacques Cauvin offers another idea, at least with regard to the Near East. In excavating the Mureybet site in Syria, he noted that the passage from the hunting-fishing-gathering system to the "wheat fields" system was immediately preceded by other changes. On the one hand, female statuettes, previously unknown, began to appear; on the other hand, inhabitants of this site began to place the skulls and horns of bulls inside the walls of their houses. Only then did they begin to change their way of life. These changes seem to herald what would later become the religion of the peasants all around the Mediterranean and beyond: a great goddess and her companion, the bull-god. This religion originated at this time. And so the first great economic revolution could have had its beginning in a religious revolution.

▲ This adze (type of axe)
▲ made of flint has been
▲ dated at 9,000 years.

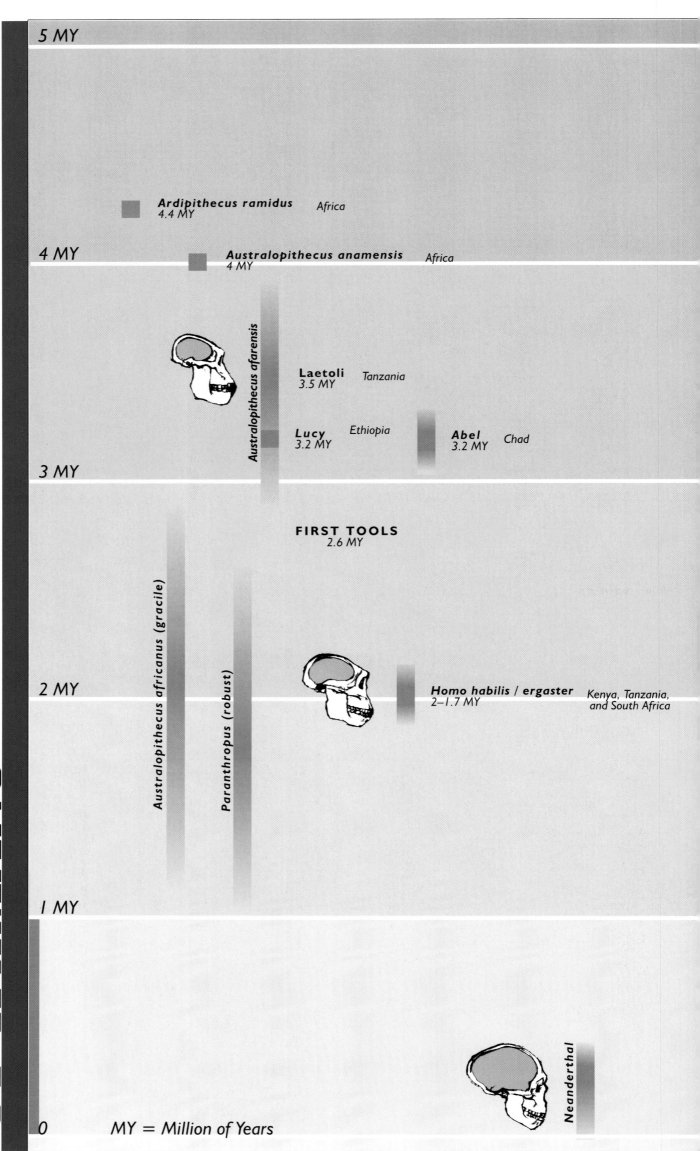

THE ORIGINS **OF HUMANS**

5 MY

Ardipithecus ramidus
4.4 MY
Africa

4 MY

Australopithecus anamensis
4 MY
Africa

Australopithecus afarensis

Laetoli
3.5 MY
Tanzania

Lucy
3.2 MY
Ethiopia

Abel
3.2 MY
Chad

3 MY

FIRST TOOLS
2.6 MY

Australopithecus africanus (gracile)

Paranthropus (robust)

2 MY

Homo habilis / ergaster
2–1.7 MY
Kenya, Tanzania, and South Africa

1 MY

Neanderthal

0   *MY = Million of Years*

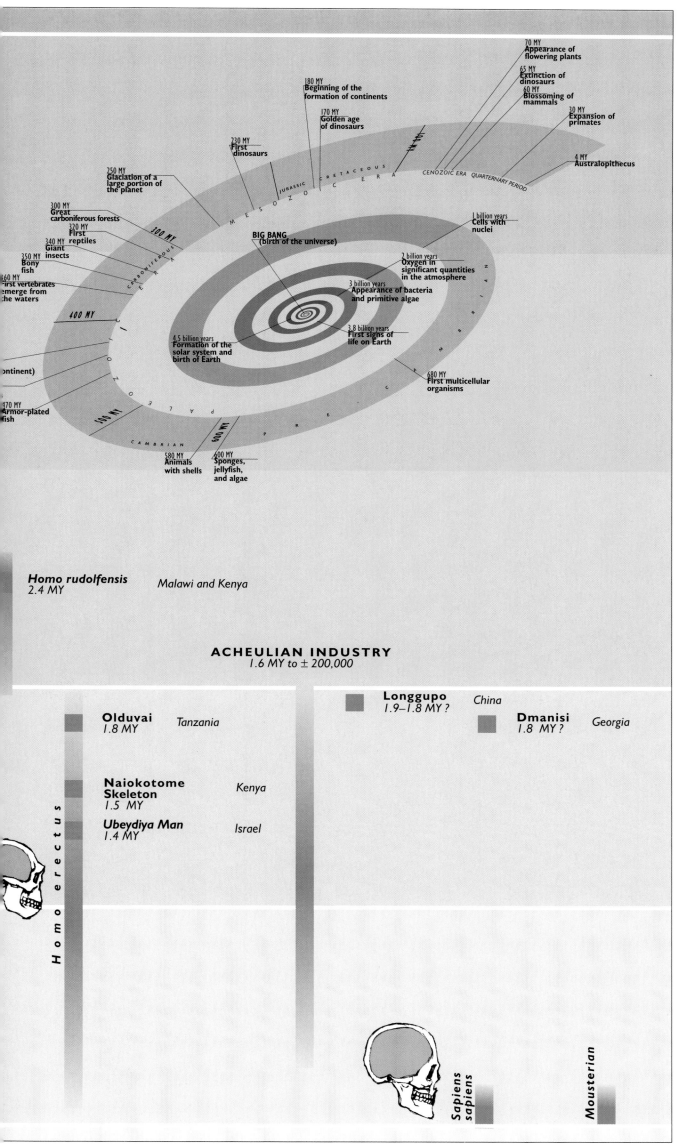

70 MY
Appearance of
flowering plants

65 MY
Extinction of
dinosaurs

60 MY
Blossoming of
mammals

30 MY
Expansion of
primates

180 MY
Beginning of the
formation of continents

170 MY
Golden age
of dinosaurs

230 MY
First
dinosaurs

4 MY
Australopithecus

250 MY
Glaciation of a
large portion of
the planet

300 MY
Great
carboniferous forests

320 MY
First
reptiles

340 MY
Giant
insects

350 MY
Bony
fish

360 MY
First vertebrates
emerge from
the waters

CENOZOIC ERA   QUARTERNARY PERIOD

1 billion years
Cells with
nuclei

BIG BANG
(birth of the universe)

2 billion years
Oxygen in
significant quantities
in the atmosphere

3 billion years
Appearance of bacteria
and primitive algae

3.8 billion years
First signs of
life on Earth

4.5 billion years
Formation of the
solar system and
birth of Earth

(ontinent)

470 MY
Armor-plated
fish

680 MY
First multicellular
organisms

580 MY
Animals
with shells

600 MY
Sponges,
jellyfish,
and algae

100 MY · 400 MY · 500 MY · 600 MY

MESOZOIC ERA · JURASSIC · CRETACEOUS · CARBONIFEROUS · PALEOZOIC · CAMBRIAN · PRECAMBRIAN

Homo rudolfensis
2.4 MY

Malawi and Kenya

ACHEULIAN INDUSTRY
1.6 MY to ± 200,000

Longgupo
1.9–1.8 MY ?

China

Dmanisi
1.8 MY ?

Georgia

Olduvai
1.8 MY

Tanzania

**Naiokotome
Skeleton**
1.5 MY

Kenya

Ubeydiya Man
1.4 MY

Israel

Homo erectus

Sapiens sapiens

Mousterian

1 MY

Soleihac *France*
900,000

Atapuerca (Gran Dolina) *Spain*
800,000

Ceprano *Italy*
700,000

Mauer
between 600,000 and 500,000 *Germany*

500,000
USE OF FIRE AND FIRST HUTS

Tautavel *France*
400,000

Terra Amata • **first fireplaces** *France*
400,000

Atapuerca (Sima de los Huesos) *Spain*
300,000

Archaic Homo sapiens
around 150,000

0

60,000

Kebara *Israel*
60,000

Shanidar *Iraq*
60,000

Jinmium *Australia*
ca. 60,000

La Chapelle-aux-Saints / La Ferrassie *France*
ca. 50,000

40,000

Chauvet Cave *France*
ca. 31,000

Swabian Jura Statuettes *France*
32,000

Cosquer Cave *France*
26,000 / 27,000

Gargas Cave *France*
27,000

LAST NEANDERTHALS
ca. 27,000

Brassempouy *France*
ca. 25,000

20,000

Lascaux *France*
15,000

Altamira *Spain*
14,000

BEGINNINGS OF AGRICULTURE IN THE NEAR EAST

Niaux *France*
11,000

FIRST DOMESTICATED PLANTS IN THE ANDES

E N D   O F   T H E

Cultures of Clovis/Folsom *United States*
8,000

0

"Roger," Boxgrove tibia
ca. 500,000   England

BEGINNING OF THE LAST GLACIATION
ca. 100,000

First humans in Australia
ca. 100,000
                Qafzeh • first burial places   Israel
                90,000

                                                    Aurignacian
                                                    38,000–27,000

                                                    Castelperronian
                                                    35,000–30,000

                        Monte Verde   Chile
                        32,000
Mungo Lake fossils   Australia   **Pedra Furada**   Brazil
30,000   30,000
            Apollo XI   Namibia   **Gravettian**
            27,000   27,000–21,000

Sungir Burial Places   Russia   **Solutrean**
ca. 21,000   21,000–17,000

                                                                         Magdalenian
                                                                         17,000–9,500
                        Meadowcroft   United States
                        13,000
Jômon Pottery   Japan   **BEGINNINGS OF THE CONQUEST OF THE ARCTIC**
ca. 10,000
    Fishing villages   South America
    ca. 10,000

L A S T   G L A C I A T I O N

                                        ca. 9,500

    Great lakes in the Sahara   Africa
    8,000

WHAT A STRANGE STORY!

Thus the "prehistory of hunters" comes to an end. Another age would begin throughout a large part of the world: that of production. After all, 2,490,000 years (or thereabouts) had already passed since the species of *Homo* first entered the scene. Only 10,000 years remained to reach the present. Indeed, almost all of human history has elapsed. So we can stop, we can also turn back to take a look at this immense and distant past. What a strange story!

It might never have taken place. The prehistory of our prehistory began in the thick shadow of the dinosaurs, and only an unpredictable planetary catastrophe gave it its initial chance. And then . . . . Well, a whole series of bizarre details were needed before we (that is, our first human ancestors) could exist. It was necessary to pass by way of the trees and, it would seem, to spend a great deal of time there. The prehistory of our prehistory thus took place in the shadow of leaves . . . and, once again, everything could have stayed there. To get things moving again, we needed another external accident—climatic. The increasing aridity in Africa these last millions of years forced some of these arboreal primates to take a chance in the savannas, and so was responsible for giving birth to the family of hominids of which we are, today, the last and only representatives. We have not always been alone. Two million years ago four rather different species of hominids coexisted in Africa. One hundred thousand years ago, two, three, or more still survived. What happened? We do not know. Why was it that only our form survived? We do not know this, either. Few paleontologists would risk saying that we were the best. The history of life (and this we now know) was in large part the result of chance.

We do know that for the last 30,000 years, anatomically modern humans have been the only hominid species. We have survived our share of catastrophes and even, it appears, prospered. But let us beware: Accidents can still occur. We have, moreover, become completely capable of producing them ourselves. Who knows if, in our shadow, a group of beings, beyond suspicion and apparently without a predictable future, is not ready to take advantage of some fatal error?

Acheulian
The name of one of the oldest stone tool industries, of which the biface is particularly representative. This industry lasted for more than one million years, beginning in Africa, then moving to Asia and to Europe.

Adapides
A group of fossil animals from America, dating back to the first part of the Tertiary period. These small climbing animals are some of the first primates.

Aurignacian
The site of Aurignac (Haute-Garonne, France) gave its name to the first group of tools (or industry) connected with modern humans in Europe.

Australopithecus
A fossil genus characterized by bipal primates that diverged from the ape lineage around 507 million years ago. Along with the genus *Homo,* it makes up the family of hominids. It has been found only in Africa.

Biface
Tool of the Acheulian industry. Completely worked on both of its two faces, it generally takes the shape of an almond. It appeared in Africa more than 1.5 million years ago and was still being made 50,000 years ago.

Bone
Along with teeth, bones are most often all that remains of the living beings of prehistory.

Châtelperonian
A rather developed industry contemporary with the Aurignacian and Cro-Magnon man that is named for a site in the center of France. This industry was also practiced by some of the last Neanderthals.

Child
It was with the skull of an australopithecine child (approximately five years old) that in 1924 the discovery of the oldest stages of human development began. The most complete skeleton of *Homo erectus* is that of a thirteen-year-old child. There are many remains of Neanderthal children. And the tombs of Grimaldi (France) and Sungir (Russia) demonstrate that prehistoric children could, upon their death, receive as many honors as adults.

Core
Block of stone prepared for making flakes.

Dating
There are two types of dating techniques: absolute and relative. Absolute dating, such as potassium argon, thermoluminescence, and carbon, have made it possible to date the fossil record. Relative dating refers to basic stratigraphy techniques of sediment superposition.

DNA
DNA contains the genetic information that makes it possible for organisms to develop, grow, and function. DNA is located in the nucleus of cells in every living organism. The analysis of the DNA of several groups of primates has specifically made it possible to detail the evolution of modern humans.

Flake
Product or by-product from the knapping of stone.

Flint
Siliceous rock existing in the form of nodules, in limestone, in clay, or in chalk. Flint was much sought after by prehistoric man. The varieties are well known, making it possible for prehistorians to locate precisely the provenance of the cut stones.

Fossil
The remains of living beings in which the components of the earth have gradually replaced the organic materials. Remains found in excavations are generally fossils.

Gathering
Grasses, fruits, and grains must have made up a large portion of the prehistoric diet. Less prestigious than hunting, gathering must nevertheless have been one of the most important activities.

Glaciation
Initially, four major glaciation events were described. Today more than twenty glacial episodes have been identified over the last 2 million years, through the analysis of core sediments removed from the ocean floor and from polar ice.

Gravettian
Second industry of the Upper Paleolithic in Europe. It followed the Aurignacian and preceded both the Magdalenian and the Solutrean.

Homo
Zoological genus of which humans are currently the sole representatives. Distinctive characteristics are a well-developed skull and brain (at least 48.8 cu. in., or 800 cm³ originally, 79.3–85.4 cu. in. or 1300–1400 cm³ today), lighter jaws, an upright posture, and a striding gait.

Hunting
Humans must have long been scavengers rather than hunters, but the new hunting weapons invented during the Upper Paleolithic made it possible to hunt with profitable results.

Industry
Group of worked stones characteristic of a period and a region.

Knapping
Way of working stone in prehistory. Several methods existed, such as hard hammer and soft hammer techniques. Flint or obsidian can be cut using pressure or using direct or indirect percussion.

Levallois
Sophisticated method of knapping stone based on the careful preparation of a core and the predetermination of pieces to be obtained. Originating much earlier than modern humans, it dates back more than 400,000 years and was used by the Neanderthals to make tools.

Magdalenian
Industry at the end of the Ice Age in Europe. This is the period in which the caves of Lascaux, Altamira, and Niaux were decorated.

Mammals
One of the zoological classes of subbranches of vertebrates. Characteristics common to mammals are the existence of hair, nursing of young, live births with no outer shells, and being warm blooded.

Mousterian
Very diverse industry associated with the Neanderthals in Europe and in the Near East, but also, in the latter region, with the first modern humans. It includes points, scrapers, often bifaces, and "Levallois" pieces.

Obsidian
Type of glass or igneous rock of volcanic origin. A marvelous material for cutting, obsidian was widely used in the Aegean region, the Near East, North America, and the Far East.

Olduvai
Celebrated paleontological and prehistoric site in Tanzania. Thanks to the work of Louis and Mary Leakey, it was the basis for the renewal of research on the origin of humans in the 1950s and 1960s.

Omomyides
One of the two oldest groups of fossil primates. Consisting of small climbing animals, it developed in Africa at the beginning of the Tertiary period.

Paleolithic
The Paleolithic (Greek word that means ancient stone) covers almost all of human history. It is generally divided into three very irregular periods: Lower, Middle, and Upper. It is the last part, and the shortest (35,000–40,000 years), that has provided us with the most information.

Pollen
Pollen from flowers can be preserved in fossil form for a long time. Collected from sediments and analyzed, it is possible to know which plants grew during a given period. By moving from one stratum to the next, it is possible to use pollen to tell the story of the vegetation at a given site; it thus becomes an aid in establishing chronologies.

Prehistory
The word prehistory is applied to all periods before recorded history, that is, before writing.

Primates
Primates are one of the twenty zoological orders that make up the class of mammals.

Quarternary
Last geological period, the Quarternary is also by far the shortest. It is, in fact, an extension of the Tertiary period with which it has an artificial border. It is currently placed at 1.8 million years, a period in which a magnetic inversion took place.

Rift
Valleys or gorges called "rifts" correspond to zones in which the earth's crust cracked, forming two distinct plates, and that separated in places where there was only one plate. A new crust was thus created, from the depths. Most often, rifts are found in oceans, but some exist on the continents, particularly in eastern Africa and in Iceland.

Rupestrian
From the Latin rupes: rock. Rupestrian art is that seen on the walls of caves or on certain stones. It is also known as "parietal" art (from the Latin paries, wall).

Sediment core sample
Column removed by a special device from the sediments (on land or at sea) in marsh peat or in the ice. The successive layers can be distinguished and analyzed.

Sediments
Long considered as the simple remains of packing, sediments have been shown to contain lots of other information and have themselves become objects of research. By their texture, their composition, and even their color, they can tell us a great deal about the past environment and climate.

Solutrean
Localized industry in the center and south of France and in the north of Spain during the Upper Paleolithic. It is distinguishable from others by its magnificent worked pieces, such as the "laurel leaf points."

Tertiary
As its name indicates, this is the third geological period. It begins after the climatic catastrophe that marked the end of the Mesozoic era, 65 million years ago.

Venus
Name or surname give to the female figurines of the European Upper Paleolithic. A distinction is made between the amply proportioned Venuses of the Gravettian and those more slender examples that were created afterward.

Wood
The oldest remains of cut wood are hunting spears that date back 400,000 years (Shoningen, Germany). The wood, which until now was obviously poorly preserved, was certainly the basic material throughout all of prehistory.